LIKE FRESH OIL

How Pain Breeds Purpose

A Memoir

Ceairia LaShay Perry
YOU DON'T KNOW THE COST OF THE OIL

©Copyright 2025 Ceairia LaShay Perry

All rights reserved. This book is protected under the copyright laws of the United States of America.

ISBN-13: 979-8-9922838-4-6

No portion of this book may be reproduced, distributed, or transmitted in any form, including photocopying, recording, or other electronic or mechanical methods, without the written permission of the publisher, except in the case of brief quotations embodied in reviews and certain other non-commercial uses permitted by copyright law. Permission granted on request.

Table of Contents

Dedication v

Introduction vi

The Source of My Existence 5

Remembering 11

Giving Myself Grace. 30

Staying in the Presence of God. 40

Take "Her" Off a Pedestal 48

The Role I Played in Suffering 58

Love is Letting Go 70

Walking in Purpose 81

Harboring Secrets. 88

Surrendering to the Mercy of God. 96

Nurturing. 103

Not Abandoning Wisdom. 116

"She" Deserved It 126

Acceptance 135

Protection 141

Forgiveness 151

Showing the World Who I Really Am. 161

Higher Standards 169

Proclaiming that I am Free 179

Witnessing God 185

Words from the Author. 195

About the Author 197

References 198

Dedication

To my sweet Symone,

You fill my heart with joy. The Lord knew exactly what I needed when He gave me, you. I knew that God loved me, and His faithfulness was evident. You, Symone, are a manifestation of a promise that God made to me, years before your conception. You are a miracle. You are special. You are mine.

Symone, as you grow and experience life, I need you to understand that some people are only in our lives for a season. Not everyone is meant to stay forever. Sometimes, God allows people to enter our lives for a specific purpose, enabling us to assist them during that season and vice versa. As people go, please accept it and be okay with where you stand. Always remember that as you encounter people every day, be intentional about making a positive impact, and always let your light shine. That way, if you ever need to reach back, you can because that person has seen nothing but goodness in you.

I love you, my sweet Symone.

Introduction

When I was four years old, I had a dream. I dreamt that I was in a secret place. This secret place was in the basement of the "family house" in a hidden corner, but it was elevated like a loft or an attic. I had to climb a ladder to get inside. This place was small, dark and desolate with only a cot, blanket, and a small light that shined just bright enough for me to see the lines of my notepad. This place was my haven. This was my sacred place, because it was here that God met me. Pen and paper in hand. This was the place where my thoughts were captured, my imagination transformed, and my emotions were validated. My young age was of no relevance.

I can recall when I was a child sitting on the front porch of the "family house" with my Aunty. She suffered from chronic muscle spasms. I remember watching her toes curl as her muscles tightened and seeing wrinkles in her forehead that read agony, deep breaths as she tried to muster through the pain. Seemed like the discomfort was relentless. One day, she told me, "Go

INTRODUCTION

upstairs, look on my dresser, and grab my blessed oil." I did as I was told. When I came back down, she said, "Here, rub some of this on your hands. Put your hands on my leg and pray." I did as I was commanded, without fear. I had never done that before. Moments after I finished praying, I watched as the muscles in her toes released, her breathing regulated. God had used me to do His work, and my young age was of no regard. Aunty said, "CeCe, you have the gift of healing." I had no idea what that meant, but I do now.

I was raised in a Christian denomination and was taught to treat everyone with respect and dignity. I often heard sayings like, "If you don't have anything nice to say, don't say it at all," or "Don't judge a book by its cover." These sayings helped shape my perception of people and how to treat others. I believe that we are all made in the image and likeness of God the Creator, so to treat anyone with ill intent is treating God in such a manner. I have always believed that, regardless of your race, ethnicity, age, disability, or gender, we all serve a purpose that was predestined from the beginning of time. It takes all kinds of people to make the world go round. Although my beliefs are rooted in Christian principles, I believe that there are some truths shared among all religions, and the common ground is rooted in love. Even a person who doesn't believe in any form of religion or doesn't practice faith requires and desires love. Some people may not share the same principles or values, but we share the common need for love, dignity, and respect.

But assuredly, God is love, and if you have ever experienced any form of love, you have experienced God. We all need care and nurturing. We all share similar experiences, and we all share a need to heal. Healing differs from person to person, but it is undoubtedly a universal experience.

The words you are about to read are true events, my life experiences, actual spiritual encounters, and revelations. Allow your mind to shift from shallow and take a deep dive with me as I take you on my healing journey.

If you have been sexually molested or experienced any form of sexual abuse, keep reading. If you grew up without a father or an inconsistent father, keep reading. If you have ever decided that abortion was your only option, keep reading. If you have buried a child, keep reading. If you have ever dealt with depression or had suicidal thoughts, keep reading. If you have been abandoned or betrayed, keep reading. If you have self-doubts, low self-esteem, or carry unforgiveness, keep reading. If you have been in an abusive relationship, keep reading. If you strive to build a closer relationship with God, keep reading.

Each chapter was intentionally designed not to include too much detail, leaving a pathway for discussions. This book serves as the framework for my ministry and will be utilized in women's support groups, seminars, and wellness retreats. It is my goal to expound on the many relatable topics hidden inside.

INTRODUCTION

At the end of each chapter, you will find reflection questions. Take some time to reflect on your own experiences, as they could relate to mine. Be open and honest with yourself. This is a safe space.

Healing was understanding where the source of my existence came from.

The Source of My Existence

"I am the Lord, your healer."
Exodus 15:26

When I think about "healing," I visualize a sore or wound that's open, infected, bleeding, or painful. It may require nurturing to mend the cells back together, repair the injured tissue, or restore a limb to good health after it has been broken.

If God created man from the dust of the ground and breathed into him the breath of life, if God can take a rib from Adam to create a woman, and if we were made in the image and the likeness of God; if God can raise Lazareth from the dead, and if Jesus can heal a man from leprosy, or heal a withered hand; if He can restore sight to the blind, or can make a lame man walk, then clearly God is the source of our healing. Right?

If you had an invention or a great phenomenon that you wanted to introduce to the world, and you are confident that the world would be a better place with your creation because many people are interested in your invention and curious to learn more about how it works. Doesn't it make sense to go directly to you, the inventor, or to simply read the manual? You know all about your creation because you put in it everything that it possesses. Right?

Let's look at it from a different perspective; you gave birth to a child. You have created this child. You have carried this child in your loins. You have nurtured this child. You have studied this child. You have invested a great deal of time and energy into caring for this child. You know his needs, and his wants. You know his cry, you know what each cry means. You can even understand his babble. When your child is sick or suffering from pain, you understand what it takes to make it all right. Right?

Well, this is exactly how it is with God. God took His time to create us. He uniquely and strategically sculpted out every molecule that makes us who we are. Every atom is bonded together to form everything from our cells to our tissues, organs, personalities, and mindsets. He is a master craftsman, qualified to heal us in every area of our lives. Our creator is ready, willing, and able to give us everything that we need. *He created us.* We make errors when we fail to acknowledge the source of our existence. We cannot heal when we fail to acknowledge the source of our existence. God.

Science is the world's way of keeping up with God. A doctor who can tap into the creation of God can only do so because he was divinely instructed by the Creator Himself.

Reflection Question: What areas of your life need healing? Whether it's mental, physical, or emotional. Dig deep to know the healing you need from your creator.

_____
_____
_____
_____
_____
_____
_____
_____
_____
_____
_____
_____
_____
_____
_____
_____
_____
_____
_____
_____

LIKE FRESH OIL

Healing was remembering.

Trigger Warning

This chapter contains content that might be troubling to some readers, including, but not limited to, memories of sexual abuse, childhood trauma, brandishing a firearm, threats, intimidation, and depictions of child pornography. Please be mindful of these and other possible triggers and seek assistance if needed.

Remembering

"Abuse keeps affecting you until you deal with it, even when you don't realize it."
Unknown.

*C*ravis:

The experience of remembering abuse and trauma varies greatly from survivor to survivor. However, I have always remembered my abuse. Over the years, I may have minimized its importance, denied its impact, or become numb to the feelings. The memories come in fragments, and it is sometimes hard to place each act in chronological order, but I have never forgotten the events themselves.

Pivotal moments in my healing journey were times spent in therapy. When I made the conscious decision to seek help, I learned that the first step to my healing was to understand how to take care of eight-year-old CeCe. I couldn't understand how to tap into this prerequisite. I prayed for wisdom and clarity, asking God to reveal to me what this meant and to remove the scales from my eyes because I knew that whatever this process entailed, it would be a significant part of my healing.

Eight-year-old CeCe was sweet and loving, paying attention to her surroundings; I was a quiet observer. I understood a lot and was introverted and well-behaved. Raised in a religious family, I was taught as a young child that "children should be seen, not heard" and to "stay in a child's place." Any form of self-defense was considered disrespectful, and self-expression was frowned upon. If you had any qualms about an elder, you were considered an "ignorant little girl."

It was this type of ludicrous mindset in child rearing that conditioned my mouth to be silent because my perpetrator was much older than I was. Cravis, my cousin, was seventeen years old when he preyed on me—time after time, taking pleasure in my childlike and innocent touch. Cravis forced me repeatedly to perform sexual acts on him. I can remember the feeling of his erect penis in the palm of my little hand—the veins. I remember the feeling of his fingers intruding down the crotch of my pants. I remember the dark rooms. I remember the disgusting smell of his spit as he put his tongue in my mouth. I remember sitting on that dingy orange carpet watching The Simpsons on that box television that sat on the floor that needed wire plyers to turn the channel while he violated my not-yet-developed breasts. I remember being forced to the basement where his drum set was and being made to "stroke this dick" while he practiced for church service. I remember every time he tried to penetrate me. My child mind didn't understand what he was trying to accomplish by doing that. I'll spare you all the disgusting details because it would make you vomit.

I sang in the church choir. I remember needing to use the bathroom. I was told to, "go on down and come right back." As I walked out of the bathroom and headed for a drink of water at the fountain, I was met by Cravis, who startled me. I then realized he followed me. From that day forward, the church was no longer a safe space for me after he forced his hand down my skirt past my pantyhose, like a fiend who couldn't resist the urgency.

The day that my mother finally found out what Cravis was doing to me was the day she walked into the room while he was on top of my little body—he molested me for almost four years. Her countenance had fallen into anger. Between the flares of her nostrils, tightly wrinkled lips, and the grit of her teeth, it assured me that she was about to hightail me far away from that place to protection quickly.

Cravis was beaten in discipline by his father's fist. It was as if my eyes were blinded to it because I couldn't recall the punches or the screams, only the words shared by my mother in a memory. However, I was wrong to anticipate protection. After Cravis had endured a brutal beating, my mother looked at me and said, "Now it's your turn. You let me walk in on that. You didn't tell me." She did not protect me; instead, she beat me with a belt. She didn't hold me in her arms or comfort me; she inflicted physical pain on me and blamed me for the abuse that I endured.

I screamed in agony at each whip to my body. I was utterly helpless and felt embarrassed as they stood like spectators and watched me squirm in pain.

Between the physical agony that I endured at the hands of my mother and the spiritual and mental affliction that Cravis caused, after Mama beat me with that leather belt, I mentally and emotionally withdrew. She never learned the whole truth about how long Cravis had molested me, and I couldn't explain how he silenced me. I remember Cravis's threats to kill my mother if I told: the intimidation, the bullying, the aggression, and that menacing phone call.

He had called the house; my Mama answered the phone, and he acted like he just wanted to say, "Wassup." He asked to speak to me, and she handed over the phone with no hesitation. He said, "My Mama told me that y'all are coming over here today. When you get here, we gon' play house again. I'll be the husband, and you'll be the wife; you have to do what I tell you to do." He was a sick dude. When I think about eight-year-old CeCe, I just want to give that little girl a hug, because she went through so much.

I remember that house, every inch of it.

That house:

The "family house". The insurmountable amount of sin, pain, and trauma that lies in the cracks and crevices of that house is enough to make God cringe. I recall listening to stories throughout the years. Stories that my greats spoke of being beaten with tree limbs and leather straps and called derogatory names like "Heffer." Being forced to crawl on their hands and knees, one child on each end, down a long wooden hallway, made to kiss one another as they crossed paths. This was a form of punishment whenever they fought or had a disagreement—hearing stories of how a drunk uncle had to be carried inside to a bathtub full of cold water to bring him back to life. Spewing out of his mouth the foulest language to his sons, the boys were beaten so severely that they prayed to the Heavens for a way out, with no intention of returning.

I can remember seeing blood drops on the floor as I listened to my uncle's bash bats against flesh. Violence and rage filled bloodstreams. Fear, anger, and rage were second nature from the oldest down to the youngest. A child so fearful of discipline that he jumped out of the third-story window. Suicidal thoughts and actions permeated cycles of hopelessness, death, addiction, depression, and loneliness. Every room in this house held unpleasant memories.

I carried aching memories silently for thirty years, not knowing that incest, child molestation, rape, sexual assault, and mental illness were handed down from generation to generation. Here I was thinking that I was alone; the whole time, the innocence of many women in my family had been stripped from them, too. Teachings like "What happens in this house stays in this house" and "Don't snitch on your family." Silence and secrets were buried in graves as if Christ didn't have the power to resurrect them.

At the beginning of my healing journey, remembering consumed me. I was swept up in a whirlwind of emotions as I relived the moments of my abuse; I had new images every day. Remembering sexual abuse or any traumatic event is not like remembering ordinary, non-threatening experiences. When traumatic memories resurface, they often appear distant and hazy. Some memories are in black and white, blurred or distant, and observed from a distance. Some memories I see from above, looking down, while others are so close I could touch them. Sometimes, memories are like being at one end of the tunnel; that's because I literally left my body at the scene. This was my brain's trauma response in creating physical distance between me and what was going on.

I don't always remember the events leading up to the abuse or what took place right afterward. I remember asking myself a lot, "Where is my Mama, and when will she be back to get me?" Some memories were so obscured that I sometimes questioned the validity of what I saw. Sometimes, a particular touch, smell, or taste triggers a memory. Sometimes memories would come to me when I was making love to my man. These types of memories were intrusive and overwhelming.

Self-care and nurturing are critical components in the stage of remembering. There may be times when memories are devastating; these are the moments when you must comfort yourself. If you feel like a memory is on the way, find a safe space, don't resist it. Remember that it's only a memory; learn how to cope with it and reach out for support.

Keith:

When I was thirteen, my mother met a man named Keith. She had joined an online dating site that a coworker had been raving about. From the beginning, I remember telling her that it was weird and that she should leave it alone. She would read off the men's profiles and ask my opinion about them. I would say, "No!" to all of them. I recall thinking, "I feel like a grown man should have better things to do with his time besides sitting on a computer meeting women." That's how I processed it as a kid.

In adolescence, I began displaying acting-out behaviors by sneaking a boy into the house. Between the 12-hour night shift that my mother worked at the hospital and spending the other nights at Keith's house, it seemed like she was barely at home. The time she spent at home was often spent sleeping, preparing for work, or recovering from work. I was an unsupervised teen in an era when I needed my mother and certainly needed parental supervision.

I felt so alone. I was experiencing puberty and hormonal changes that I could not understand, along with new emotions that I had never experienced before. I just wanted my Mama, but even when she was there, she wasn't present. I ran away from home. I wrote a runaway letter and left that morning while my mother slept in the next room. It wasn't long before I was found and brought back home.

I can remember how upset and worried my family was. My uncles spoke sensibly in making me realize how unsafe and unnecessary running away was, and my aunts were levelheaded women who tried to convey to me never to do that again. But Keith, on the other hand, I remember pulling me off to the side. He said, "I'm glad you're back home, but I understand why you did what you did. One day, your body will develop into a beautiful woman, then you can do whatever you want." I didn't think anything of what he said. It wasn't until later in life that I remembered it and realized how inappropriate it was for him to make comments about my body developing. We didn't have the type of relationship that allowed him to say anything of that sort to me. Now, I understand his motivation for choosing those words at that moment.

Keith seemed very eerie to me from the jump. He had a paralyzing stutter that hindered his speech. They had dated for some months, and it wasn't long before he had the key to our house and the free will to do as he pleased. It seemed like he came from out of nowhere and rapidly took over our lives. Keith somehow convinced my mother to sell her house and downsize to a home that he had strategically purchased in only his name. I honestly don't know what my mother saw in that man. He had rotten teeth and carried a type of arrogance that I suppose came from pride in being a law enforcement officer.

I worked with Tina. Tina was a beautiful young lady with dark chocolate melanin skin.

Tina was a mother of two girls. Over the years, we built a working relationship that evolved into a personal one. Tina came to me one evening to let me know that we would no longer be working together, as she needed to adjust her hours to be home with her children. I recall the passion in her tone when she spoke about her girls reaching an age where it was mandatory for her to be home with them, especially at night. "Girl, the things that happen at night. The things that kids can get into at night, I need to be home with my girls. Cause if something happens to my kids while I'm at work, I would never be able to forgive myself." I admired that about Tina. This was well into my adult years, but as I reflect, I wish my mother had prioritized me in that way. I hated that Mama worked the night shift!

A little while later, my mom and Keith got married. At this point, I had no other choice but just to accept the relationship for what it was. So, I guess it's safe to say we had a cool relationship, despite my gut feelings.

When we moved into the new house, they had designated my room to be in the finished basement, which sat adjacent to Keith's man cave. I never felt comfortable sleeping in my room; it was too close to where he lounged. He could easily look in on me as I lay in my bed. I always had an uneasy feeling about being down there, with him, even with the door closed. Instead, I chose to sleep on the top bunk bed with my younger brother on the lower one. I felt safer there.

Two years into their marriage, I was fifteen. I'd just made the varsity cheerleading team and been named team captain. The school hosted an honors ceremony, where trophies and letters for our letterman jackets were presented to all the athletes. I was extremely proud of myself for being selected as squad captain. My father attended the ceremony, but this was the first time I had seen him in years. My mother was unable to attend the ceremony due to work, and Keith didn't come because my father would be there.

That night, I was sleeping when Keith came into the bedroom. He woke me up with a gun pointed at me. "Get up. I wanna take some pictures of you," he said with a stutter. My heart pounded, and I couldn't utter a sound. I climbed down from the bed, trying hard not to wake up my brother. He made me go into the living room, and he started taking off my clothes. He walked to the dining room table and grabbed the letter "B," which I was awarded just a few hours before. I had laid it on the dining room table before I went to bed for my Mama to see it when she came home from work that next morning.

Keith forced me to pose nude as he took pornographic pictures of me. He enjoyed every second of it. It seemed that in his sin-sick and twisted mind, he was pretending to be a professional photographer, asking his client to pose for different shots. "Put your hand here, put your left leg there, open your legs a little wider. Bend over. Put your head up and wipe your face," he said. After about thirty minutes, he told me to go back to bed. I ran. Keith came back five minutes later, saying, "I didn't get the shot I was looking for," and he made me come back. I was helpless. I went back by his command in fear for my life. He took more photos. He didn't finish with me until he was completely satisfied.

Just like Cravis, Keith threatened to kill my mother if I told. "Don't tell ya Mama. If you do, imma kill her. You wouldn't want to be the cause of the family breaking up." So, there I was again, defenseless because these men knew my weakness. They used the love I had for my mother as a tool to abuse and silence me. They knew our relationship, how much I adored my mother, and that I would do absolutely anything to protect her.

I started sleeping on the couch by the front door. It was the nearest exit, and I promised myself that if he ever tried anything like that again, I would run straight out that door and wouldn't come back. I slept on that couch from my sophomore year until I graduated from high school.

Soon after I graduated, Keith and my mom separated. I have no recollection of what caused the separation, but I was relieved that she had escaped that man. I knew who he really was and what he was capable of. I was just glad that he was out of our lives. My mother had moved into her own apartment, doing well and managing life independently with her children.

Some months later, she let Keith back into our lives. I remember the moment I heard him walk into our apartment. I was afraid, and devastation made my blood boil; every fiber of my being cringed. I locked myself in the bathroom; I sat on the floor, curled in a fetal position, trembling; my heart was pounding uncontrollably. Mama had been calling my name to come down and greet him, but I couldn't; I was petrified because he was a monster in my eyes.

Keith taunted me. Those early mornings, he would come to my school, leaving silent threats. The looks he gave me from the rear-view mirror during family outings that my mother was completely unaware of, as well as the intimidating glares he would cast across the room. The fabrication that he told my mother about me tampering with his mancave and blasting his stereo system. When I told Mama that I did no such thing, she said, "I don't believe you. I don't trust you. You made this bed now lay in it." The amount of betrayal and hopelessness that I felt at that moment was enough to make me question if she was even worth protecting anymore. Keith had managed to pit us against each other.

Keith was later diagnosed with mid-stage prostate cancer. It was like he was experiencing God's wrath for what he had done to me. When I learned about his illness, I had no remorse or pity for him. After his surgery, my mother nursed him back to health. Shortly after that, she miraculously discovered that Keith had a porn addiction after finding a collection of self-help books that he kept hidden in a secret compartment in his mancave. The day she called him out on it was the day he cowardly filed for a divorce.

"Why did Keith do that to me? What was his motive?" I asked myself. After a great deal of research and talking to a professional, I learned that Keith may have suffered from a mental illness referred to as "obsessive-compulsive disorder." It may have caused him to be fascinated with the physical development of young girls. This was why he made the inappropriate comment years prior about my body, "one day developing into a beautiful woman." I believe that Keith targeted me from the very beginning and used my mother as a cover-up for his perverse illness.

I've always been a silent observer; I paid attention to his behavior and noticed his patterns. Keith would intentionally initiate arguments with my Mama every Thursday night. I was woken up to the bellows of screaming and profanity. I would put my ear up to the wall and listen to my mother cry in the room next door. Keith either left the house or hibernated in his mancave until he was ready to come out. He manipulated his way out of her presence to be able to feed his addiction and pamper his sickness. This was the time that he created to indulge in his filth.

He had a very weird and perverse obsession, and it made no sense to me because Keith had a daughter. If only he had considered her in his actions, then maybe he could've contemplated what if someone had violated his daughter to the magnitude that he had violated me.

In school, I was taught to be cautious about what I post on the internet because it can never be erased. For many years, I wondered what Keith did with those pictures. Did he sell them on some online porn site? Did he post them somewhere for the world to see? Periodically, I would do random Google searches to see if my name or face would appear because I was concerned that my friends and family would somehow find them. When I began applying to colleges, I was anxious that recruiters would access them and deny my acceptance. When applying for careers that required extensive background checks, I was worried that I wouldn't get the job because they found those obscene nudes of me. The mental anguish that I suffered at the hands of my stepfather damaged my adolescence and spilled into adulthood.

Pause

Take a moment to regroup, because I know that I just laid some heavy stuff on you. Take a deep breath.

Be encouraged…

Anyone who has ever done you wrong.

Anyone who has hurt you.

Anyone who has made you the recipient of betrayal.

Anyone who wounded you when all you tried to share was your goodness.

Anyone who abused you and hid their sin behind a mask of righteousness

They will regret it.

You see, when the Roman Soldiers persecuted Jesus, they soon realized their wrong. But by then, it was too late, because redemption was activated. When they discovered that the flesh they crucified was a mirror of God Himself – they wallowed in regret until the day they met death.

The same scenario has played out in repeated cycles for over 2,000 years. So, do not fret, and do not be dismayed because your enemies will get all that they deserve.

That's God's promise.

"Vengeance is Mine, I will repay," says the Lord. Romans 12:19

Reflection Questions: **What is your most painful memory? Is it easy for you to remember? How do you feel inside because of that memory? Be as detailed as possible.**

_____
_____
_____
_____
_____
_____
_____
_____
_____
_____
_____
_____
_____
_____
_____
_____
_____
_____

REMEMBERING

Healing was giving myself grace.

Trigger Warning

This chapter contains content that might be troubling to some readers, including, but not limited to the loss of a child, grief, abortion and suicidal ideations. Please be mindful of these and other possible triggers and seek assistance if needed.

Giving Myself Grace

I had carried this baby boy for eight months, and I was proud to give my husband a son. I had done everything right: I finished high school, then college, and finally got married. I thought that I had done things decently and in order so that God could bless my family.

I'll never forget how active he was in my belly—always moving, always kicking. His kicks and movements were so forceful that I was sure he was a boy; the ultrasound only confirmed what I already knew. He felt like a boy. I recall being fascinated by watching my belly grow. I remember the day my belly button finally popped out, and watching my nose as it gradually spread across my face. The smell of air freshener made me sick to my stomach. I would vomit every time I ate a bag of plain Lay's potato chips, but that's what I craved the most. I had even started to recognize which foods elicited the most reaction from him. I remember how active he was at nighttime; I had so many sleepless nights because he was full of energy. The carpal tunnel in both of my hands and the pregnancy-induced sciatica had gotten so painful that some days, I had to crawl to get around.

I had constant migraines and vomiting that not even Zofran could manage. But, for him, every second of discomfort was worth it; whatever it took to get my son here, I endured. I loved him so much from the moment of his conception.

When I went in for a thirty-two-week prenatal checkup, the doctor put the fetal doppler on my protruding belly; a process that should have taken all of ten seconds took three minutes. She instructed her assistant to prepare me for an ultrasound. This was odd because my prior visit was no more than seven minutes. She escorted us to the ultrasound room. I laid on the bed in anticipation of seeing my baby, but I still didn't fully understand what was going on. My husband was by my side, standing in support. We eagerly looked up at the monitor.

It was like someone had thrown a bucket of scalding hot water all over my flesh. Devastation permeated every molecule in my body. Sadness overcame us, and tears flooded the room as we looked at his little body lying lifeless in my womb, with no movement, no activity. My soul ached, and my spirit groaned as I listened to my husband question, "Why is he not moving? What happened?" in rage and confusion. I remember staring at the screen, hoping that God would either rejuvenate his broken heart or wake me up from this nightmare.

Just a week prior, I went to see my doctor because I was concerned about the decrease in movement. I felt like something wasn't quite right. The nurse told me, "You were just here last week, and everything was fine. I'm sure the baby is good.

Around the third trimester, a baby's movement lessens because they are gaining weight and running out of room in the belly." I took her at her word and left because, what did I know? I beat myself up because I didn't speak up; I didn't advocate for myself or my baby, especially when I knew that I deserved a complete checkup that day. Instead, I let it go. I blamed myself because his death may have been prevented had I just spoken up.

I gave birth to my lifeless son thirteen hours later. I watched as my nurse came in to care for me with tears in her eyes and a warm tone that consoled me; it was like she felt my pain. I held Jr's fully developed body in my arms. I can still feel his head full of silky hair in my hands. I studied his every feature; he was a spitting image of me from head to toe. It felt like I was dying a slow and painful death. For the rest of my life, I will never forget what it felt like to leave the hospital without Jr. in my arms.

I felt like I had dropped the ball, as if this was all my fault and nothing or nobody could convince me otherwise. "My only obligation was to get this baby here healthy, and I couldn't even do that right," is what I told myself daily.

I went through a whirlwind of emotions, months of turmoil, and depression. Every emotion that God created, I suffered with in constant cycles. I resented every woman I saw, and I loathed women who I saw carrying a seed. All I wanted was to be a mother. I became obsessed with having another baby, and my mind was consumed with nothing but thoughts of motherhood. I prayed, pleaded to the heavens, and begged the universe to give me a child. My mind had become so ill that I compromised my morals and beliefs to tap into whatever other higher deity existed. If God didn't work, I asked the universe to take over; that way, I covered all the bases.

I suffered with an enormous amount of guilt. The demonic voices in my head convinced me that losing my child was punishment for secretly getting those two abortions back in college; for being so damn selfish and self-centered; for throwing those babies away like garbage with no remorse and never looking back. The demons in my head told me, "Because you chose to fornicate, this is the result of your actions. You made this bed, now lay in it." That is precisely what I did. I sank into a bottomless, dark pit of sorrow. I contemplated suicide daily, and so many irrational thoughts filled my mind. I just wanted to be with my baby, but I was unable to rationalize that if I killed myself, I would never see him again. I felt like I no longer served a purpose in this world. Every ounce of femininity that I possessed was stripped away. "I can't bear children, so what's my purpose?" I felt less of a woman, worthless.

I carried shame and embarrassment on my shoulders like the weight of the world, and I was even embarrassed for my husband. I thought that people looked at me with disgust because "stillbirth" was completely unheard of in my community. "Who in the hell doesn't know that they're carrying a dead baby?" I felt like my mother resented me for mishandling her grandbaby. Mama was the only person outside of my marriage who knew a glimpse of the toxicity that existed in my marriage. She had often expressed that she believed stress was the cause of Jr's death. Jr's umbilical cord coiled tighter than the spirals of a notebook and plunged out of his belly button. He had lost blood and oxygen supply; he lived in my obstructed placenta for weeks. My doctor had unempathetically referred to my loss as "a freak accident."

It was the smallest casket I had ever seen. It was white, polished with a symbol of a dove on the side. I couldn't believe that I went from planning my baby shower to putting my baby in a grave in a matter of days. I just wanted to crawl under a rock, but when I looked around at the many women who, too, had lost their babies, I felt comfort in knowing that I wasn't alone.

I was sitting in my bathroom, away from the world. I was in complete agony, crying and screaming out to God for mercy. The pain in my heart was unbearable. Suddenly, I felt a gentle touch on my hand; a woman appeared before me, she was dressed beautifully in all white. She was graceful. She never said a word, but she didn't need to because her presence gave me all the calm and comfort I needed.

I decided to terminate those pregnancies nine months apart from each other. My family was disappointed that I had returned home after only one semester at the university down south. They expressed their sentiments in a not-so-pleasant way. "If you keep on making these types of decisions, you're going to end up pregnant and dropping out of school," my uncle said. His words ignited a burning desire to prove him wrong; therefore, dropping out was not an option. So, when I found out that I was pregnant, both times, termination was my only option.

I walked into the clinic with one purpose in mind. My decision was made, and no one could convince me otherwise. I recall speaking to the abortion counselor, and she asked me, "Why do you feel like abortion is the best option?" I responded, "Because I'm in school, and nothing is going to stop me from finishing." I suppose she sensed the urgency in my tone, because she backed away from asking me another question. After I gowned up, they escorted me into a waiting room in the back.

Placed up against the walls were about eighteen chairs in a circle; women of all ages and nationalities filled every chair. I remember sitting there feeling mellow from the Valium the nurse had given me just minutes prior. Sitting across from me was a young girl; she was crying. I could sense that she was having second thoughts about her decision. Her tears triggered another girl; then another. Before I knew it, almost every woman in that waiting room was crying. The nurse came in, and one woman told her, "I can't do this." She left. Yet, I felt no regret about my decision. I was adamant. I didn't want a baby; I had to finish school because failure was not an option.

Nine months later, I walked into the abortion clinic, a full-circle moment. I realized that I had picked the wrong appointment day when I ran into my stepsister, who was in the waiting room, sobbing, with bellows of regret. When she noticed me, she desperately pleaded for me to leave. "Please, Ceairia, don't do this!" She had even called my older sister, who blew up my phone with texts and voice messages, pleading with me not to go through with it. I was not persuaded because I had already made up my mind. I didn't want a baby. I wanted to finish school because failure was not an option.

Life has a way of surprising us with challenges we didn't plan for and storms we didn't see coming. In those moments, remember to breathe and to give yourself grace. Grace reminds us that we don't have to have it all figured out; it's okay to get it wrong. Remember to trust God with what feels too heavy to carry. Grace invites us to be patient with ourselves while we navigate what we never expected. We are not defined by the weight of our circumstances, but by the strength we find in the Lord.

Reflection Questions: **What was your hardest loss? Describe your grieving process. Are you healing? What steps are you taking to heal?**

LIKE FRESH OIL

Healing required staying in the presence of God.

Staying in the Presence of God

"The human soul doesn't want to be advised, or fixed, or saved. It simply wants to be witnessed, to be seen, heard, and companioned exactly as it is. When we make that kind of deep bow to the soul of a suffering person, our respect reinforces the soul's healing resources, the only resource that can help the sufferer make it through."
Parker Palmer. The Gift of Presence

"Lord, I want to be so close to you that when I hear your voice, I never doubt it again." In the name of Jesus. Amen.

My Mama said, "If what you're doing ain't working, then do something different." When it came to coping with my abuse, I tried to drink the pain away; I tried to sex the pain away, but the alcohol did not work, and the sex certainly didn't change a thing. I had reached a point where all that I desired was to be in the presence of God. In this desire, I had to be intentional about turning away from sin because God could not stay in my presence and watch me indulge in drunkenness and fornication. I did not want God to turn away from me for even a second, because I understood that that one second might be the one that changed my life.

God began to deal with me concerning my personal values and convictions. When we have accepted Christ into our lives as our personal Lord and Savior, we are held to a higher standard. When the Spirit of God convicts our hearts to turn away from sin, we cannot stand before God on the day of judgment and tell Him that we didn't know. The spirit that lives within us will be a witness against us if we choose to partake in sin after being convicted. I refused to lose my salvation for fleshly pleasures.

Well after my divorce, I was no longer interested in dating or meeting new people. It was as if God had transformed my mind in an instant, giving me tunnel vision. As a result, many friends dropped off, and I was left in a world with me and Him because they could not withstand my transformation and did not understand the new language I spoke. I never knew a peace like that existed. When I thought about it transparently, I had been having sex since I was four years old. I was exhausted, and God knew exactly what I needed to replenish my strength.

I was six years old when God showed himself to me. I remember it vividly and clearly as if it were yesterday, riding in the back seat as my mom drove to work. She had worked at the center for quite some time before being transferred to a far county location. That drive seemed so long; I remember the scenery and watching the cars pass by on the freeway, taking in the world around me, the land, the green grass, and the clouds. Those clouds were so beautiful, white and fluffy, perfect in the light blue sky. As I looked toward the heavens, I saw standing on a cloud an image of a man, huge in stature, wearing a dark-colored robe; dark purple is what I believe. His presence was majestic and divine. I gazed in awe. At that moment, my age made no difference because I knew and understood exactly who I was looking at. So close yet so far; I was fearless. In that moment, God made His presence known to me.

I carried this image in my mind every day of my life, and as I began to grow and build my relationship with Christ, this memory was my redeeming quality. In every crisis I endured, I possessed the ability to look up to the face of God. He was my strength and my fortress. I was able to endure every obstacle because Christ wrapped Himself in flesh, stepped down from His throne, and came to Earth just to reveal Himself to me. It was as if, at that moment, His presence said, "I will never leave you. I will never forsake you. I will be there with you even until the end of time." Oh, how good and how faithful He is to do such a thing for little ol' me. Many people can hear from God, and some people can feel God's presence, but I was blessed with the ability to see, hear, and feel His presence.

When God showed Himself to me that day, He gave me a portion of Himself. People tell me things like, "I just like to be around you," or "You command presence when you enter a room." Friends who thought they could do without me came back desiring my presence. This is because I carry the presence of God. What people feel about me has nothing to do with me but everything to do with God. They do not desire me; they desire the presence of God that is within me. God has given me a precious gift, and He is teaching me every day how to use it.

God came to me to disrupt a generational curse. He allowed His presence to be my anchor so that I could always return to Him.

As I craved His presence more, God began to transmogrify my mind and my imagination, and I began to see things in the spirit. I began spending a significant amount of time in prayer and supplication, offering humble pleas and sincere thanks. In moments of prayer, I envisioned myself prostrate at the feet of Christ as my body had teleported to the Heavens.

In my imagination, I was the woman with the issue of blood, who was considered ceremonially unclean by Jewish law and had spent all her money on doctors who were unable to heal her. She believed that if she could touch the edge of Jesus' cloak, she would be healed. She came up from behind Jesus and touched his garment, and her bleeding stopped immediately. (Luke 8:43-48)

This story resonates with me because I sympathize with her desperation for healing. As blood gushed from my body for six constant months, pain and discomfort seized my reproductive organs. Cancer was active on my cervix, and my healthy cells began to deteriorate. After countless visits to the doctor and three surgeries later, I became the woman with the issue of blood. But just like her, in faith, I stood unshakable, trusting that Christ was the source of my strength and my healing.

I became like the Gentile Mother, who had great faith. I hungered for Him so much that I prayed, "Lord, thank you that I can even eat the crumbs from the master's table." (Mark 7:24-30).

My prayers were relentless as tears streamed from my eyes like waterfalls; I tirelessly blessed the name of the Lord while sweat poured from my pores, like fresh oil. "Lord, let my praise be a sweet-smelling aroma like the perfume poured upon your feet." I had transfigured into the Pharisee woman. (Luke 7:36-50)

Dilute the pain and do something new in me, oh Lord, because I don't want it anymore. I trust that you can do all things. Oh Lord, create in me a clean heart and renew a right spirit within me. I have stuff on the inside of me that only you, my creator, are equipped with the tools to get out of me. Lord, I die to myself. Change the momentum of my past and break the curse that has taken me captive. In the name of Jesus. Amen.

Reflection Question: Have you ever had a spiritual encounter? Explain.

LIKE FRESH OIL

Healing was learning how to take "her" off a pedestal.

Take "Her" Off a Pedestal

*"Sometimes people don't really let you down;
you just had them up too high."*
Unknown

"CeCe, you have been everyone's gatekeeper. You have protected everyone, and you have been a preserver of peace since you were four years old. You have even protected your abusers. You carried this cross and fought this silent battle with grace because you haven't hurt yourself or anybody else. As much as you strive to be like Christ, you are not equipped to carry this cross to the end. At some point, you must drop it because it will become too heavy. You have taken on the sins of those men; you were forced to relinquish your right to protection in the name of protecting "her." In the process of protecting her, you became enmeshed with her, and you placed "her" on a pedestal, almost higher than God. For your own mental health, you've gotta bring her down."

Certain people asked me how I could love my mother so deeply despite of. But what type of asinine question was that? Because how could I not devote myself to the woman who gave me life? For me, it was all hail The Queen, and there was nothing anybody could have done or said to make me feel any different. My loyalty to my mother surpassed everything.

To put something on a pedestal is to elevate it above us, to idealize it, making it unattainable. Then, I was introduced to what it means to be enmeshed. Being enmeshed with someone is defined as having an overly close and intertwined relationship where personal boundaries are blurred, leading to a lack of individual identity and a feeling of needing to constantly meet the other person's needs at the expense of your own feelings and desires.

Through self-evaluation, I discovered that this enmeshment weighed on me the most. It led me to feel like I was responsible for my mother's emotions and well-being to an unhealthy degree. My need to protect her was a fallacy based on the position I had placed her in my mind.

I struggled to identify and express my own needs and feelings. I also suffered from emotional codependency, where I relied heavily on her for emotional validation, and it was difficult for me to make decisions without consulting her. I took her criticism very personally. I sought the help of a professional to teach me how to disengage from her criticisms and skills to enhance my sense of self-worth. Although I was close to my mother, I started realizing that our relationship was not healthy because her criticisms were the only criticisms that made me feel like garbage; that made me contemplate killing myself. The magnitude to which I held her opinion was much too high. This enmeshment messed with my psyche in a way that even my man of sixteen years didn't have this effect on me. I had become so enmeshed that I walked in her purpose and lived out her dreams.

I had lost my job at the law firm and had been actively searching for a job for over six months. I was close to landing a great position at a prestigious IP law firm and was invited back for a second interview; however, the position was ultimately offered to another candidate. I worked hard to receive my master's degree, and all I wanted was to work in my field of expertise. However, after numerous interviews, I began to lose hope.

Mama and I were driving down the street one afternoon, and out of nowhere, I blurted out, "Let's open up a daycare center." She was all in. She had owned several daycares some years prior, but was forced to shut down after changes in the licensing code. Teaching was Mama's passion, and owning a thriving daycare center was her dream. So, I figured, "What better time than now to make Mama's dream come true?" Together, we hustled, built the business, and sacrificed to make provisions. However, the silent battles I fought were sometimes overwhelming because she had extensive experience in childcare, while I had none. So, when she shared her ideas or input, I often felt inferior. This was one of the biggest sacrifices of my life, but I was happy to do it for her.

Many people admired our relationship because of the bond we shared, but they never saw it behind the scenes. Being a business partner with your mother is not for the faint of heart, especially when you struggle to compartmentalize the business from the personal relationship. I felt like a lot of the calls that she made were in the name of being "the mother." Things were always a power struggle, and she always won because she held the title of, "Mama." I started accumulating a pile of mixed emotions because, at times, I felt like everything I did just wasn't good enough, like I could never do anything right.

One day, we got into a physical altercation. I can't recall what it was about, but at this point, the issue caused me to boil over, and I was filled with anger and rage. I was highly offended, but I had lost my everlasting mind. Before I knew it, we were on the floor fighting. During my rage, I heard myself screaming, "You let him hurt me! You let him hurt me!" But nothing came out of my mouth. This level of rage gave me the strength of an ox. We were exchanging blows and body shots. When I came to myself, I realized that I was fighting my mother. I had an out-of-body experience. I was fighting her for everyone who had done me wrong. My mother had not done anything to deliberately harm me, but years of hurt, pain, and resentment had built up, and I was a ticking time bomb ready to explode.

The person she truly was and the person that I created in my mind were two totally different people, and it took the help of my therapist to help me decipher the difference. I placed her in a position so high that I failed to give her grace when she made mistakes. I deprived her of humanistic qualities because, in my mind, she didn't possess the ability to do wrong, which was the reason I blamed her for my sufferings. Putting her on a pedestal prevented me from experiencing a realistic connection and from accepting her on a human level.

My mother and father divorced when I was two years old. I have no recollection of ever being with my parents in the same household. Not having a dad laid heavy on me, but as time grew, I saw for myself that they were better off apart; I understood why. I have always known who my father was, but never really knew him. I was unable to build a true daddy-daughter bond with him because he was not consistently present. The many nights he chose not to come home to us, and the many times he promised to pick me up but never showed up; he missed fragments of my life. The pop-ups were random and only at his convenience. His love for me was deep, but his infatuation with women overpowered his priorities, and his commitment to the streets were strong. His inconsistencies prevented me from experiencing what it meant to be loved and respected by a man, and his insufficiencies took away my expectation of protection.

I wish I could make a list of the wonderful things we did together or the lessons he taught me. I wish that I could remember him escorting me to school or feeding me a dose of Tylenol when I spiked a fever. I wish that he were there to protect me when wicked perverts preyed on me. I wish that he had shown me through example how my husband was supposed to treat me, because Daddy's womanizing behavior was all that I knew. I have always cherished the love that I received from him during those sporadic visits, but not to mention that during those sporadic visits, I was handed off to a stepmother who hated my existence, and she taught my older sister to do the same. Or I was dropped off with strange women and left abandoned for hours as I fearfully waited for his return. When I got older, I had to sit in the background and listen to all the great things he provided for the stepchildren that he prioritized. He purchased them cars, he took them places; the joy and memories they shared. I carried my father in my heart even in his absences, and I loved him unconditionally even through his inadequacies.

Understanding how to take my mother "off the pedestal" took weeks, and my therapist had to remind me several times because my brain wasn't grasping this concept. Suddenly, a still voice said, "You have to love her the same way that you love your father." At that moment, I realized that I didn't love her correctly, and I certainly didn't know that I had to love them the same.

Taking her off the pedestal was not to distort the relationship I had with my mother, but to create a healthy one and establish much-needed boundaries. In doing so, I was able to construct my own identity and improve my self-esteem based on my own merits. This pedestal was the most detrimental to my mental health, and learning how to "bring her down" allowed me to set my own goals and to walk into my purpose.

Reflection Questions: Do you struggle with setting boundaries? Why? What are your values? On the lines below, create a set of boundaries for yourself that align with your values.

_____
_____
_____
_____
_____
_____
_____
_____
_____
_____
_____
_____
_____
_____
_____
_____
_____
_____
_____
_____
_____

TAKE "HER" OFF A PEDESTAL

Healing was acknowledging the role that I played in my sufferings.

Trigger Warning

This chapter contains content that might be troubling to some readers, including, but not limited to, spousal abuse, domestic violence, and verbal abuse. Please be mindful of this and other possible triggers and seek assistance if needed.

The Role I Played in Suffering

You cannot pour into a broken cup!

"If every conversation about how you feel turns into an argument, you're dealing with a psychological abuser and or narcissistic personality. Expressing how you feel to a non-abuser would elicit empathy and remorse for their mistakes and an honest effort to never do it again." Unknown

When considering the role that I played in my suffering, I had to take accountability for my choices, behaviors, thought patterns, and actions that contributed to my pain and my experiences. *Negative coping mechanisms*: I used unhealthy ways to deal with stress, such as overindulging in alcoholic beverages. Drunkenness caused my behavior to spiral out of control. My drunken states were so ridiculous and premeditated that I would call to make sure my daughter was safe at home before I indulged. I was fully aware of where my mind would go and could care less where my body landed. It was in those intoxicated states that I wallowed in my sorrow and resurfaced painful memories from my past. I even acknowledged that I liked the way edibles made me feel. *Negative thought patterns:* I often engaged in self-criticism. I feared that people were always speaking against me or had a negative perception of me. *Lack of self-care:* I neglected my physical and mental health needs, which made me more vulnerable to suffering. *Avoidance behaviors:* I avoided addressing issues head-on. Instead, I would isolate myself or silence my voice. As a result, my problems festered and worsened.

Poor decision-making and ignoring red flags: Sometimes, we fail to recognize the importance of being equally yoked. We wonder why we outgrow people, why relationships don't work, and how friendships end. You must surround yourself with people who share the same beliefs and values as you.

I wish I had understood the importance of being equally yoked back then; it would have influenced my decisions for the better. I was oblivious to dating because I chose to be committed to one man for sixteen years. The puppy love was blissful, and the verbal abuse was sporadic. Then came the threats and the intimidation, but I was blinded by the shopping sprees, fine dining, and affection that he displayed in between his violent outbursts. I ignored the flinches to his raised hand and the dishes slamming as I spoke. The door that was broken in rage, the cat who suffered cruelty, the disrespect to his mother, the tantrums, and the apology speeches were all overlooked. I forgave him every time. I met him at the altar and bore his children, signed the dotted line, and intertwined our dysfunctions into a matrimony that was not so holy.

The spiritual abuse stripped away my confidence. The verbal abuse kept me silent and defenseless. The emotional abuse made me feel like I was not enough. The lies made me wonder if I was going insane. The manipulation made everyone believe that he was great. The intimidation murdered my self-esteem. The physical abuse strangled my neck, held me over the kitchen stove, ignited a fire that fully engulfed the left side of my hair, and ran away for our toddler daughter to watch me burn. I can still feel the blistering heat thrust against my face. I can still see the flames as they traveled up my freshly pressed silk locks. I can still smell the odor of burnt sulfurous acid, and I can still hear the cries of my baby screaming, "Mommy!"

Sr. and I certainly didn't share the same values or beliefs, and I hold myself accountable because I had a mother who spoke against abuse and exemplified zero tolerance for that type of nonsense. But I stayed. Determined to make my marriage work, and the feeling of obligation to uphold the vows that I made before God.

"When a person shows you who they are, believe them the first time. They know themselves much better than you do". Maya Angelou.

"If you don't stop talking, Imma ram yo' head through that wall."

"I'll slap fire from you."

"I'll beat yo' ass if you say that again."

"You think you're better than somebody, now that you have all these degrees."

"Stupid bitch."

"You can't make it without me. You need me."

"I love you to death."

I blamed myself for not believing that man…

After sixteen long years, I realized that I didn't want to be subjected to his abuse any longer, and I refused to raise my daughter with this level of toxicity. I strategically formulated a plan and got out. This is the story of many women and men, too. If you are in an abusive relationship or marriage and have a hard time getting out, I encourage you to create a strategic safety plan for escape. Effective safety plans include two different sets of steps.

1. Increasing your safety while living with your abusive partner.

    - Plan escape routes and determine where you would go if you needed to stay overnight.
    - Hide spare car keys in different places. Hide birth certificates, Social Security cards, insurance doc-

uments, and bank cards in areas where you can quickly grab them and leave.
- Get out of dangerous places during arguments, such as the kitchen, where he can grab knives or other dangerous items to hurt you.
- Obtain a private post office box for important mail.
- Come up with code words with your children, friends, and close family members that indicate an emergency.
- Open a secret bank account.
- Carry a cell phone. Ensure the battery remains charged.
- Get a permit to carry a firearm or pepper spray.
- Stay sober to make sure that your judgment is never impaired.
- Call the police if you find yourself in immediate danger.

2. After you leave your abusive partner.

- Change the locks at home.
- Inform neighbors of the danger and show them pictures of the abuser. Give descriptions of his car.
- Let your employer know of your danger.
- Teach your children not to speak to the abuser or to run for help if they see him.
- Make appropriate reports to law enforcement.
- Inform the children's school of the danger.
- Teach your children how to dial 911.
- Take different routes when you travel.

Most people who prepare a plan are successful in leaving and staying away from an abuser.

I had stooped so low and dug myself deep into a pit of disgust that I confided in a married man. The physical attraction soon turned into an emotional one. Before I knew it, my unrealistic expectations became a ridiculous obsession—this type of emotional turmoil I inflicted on myself because I knew that God disapproved. My selfishness caused me to be blind to the hurt that I inflicted on myself and others, as I ruthlessly strived to satisfy my own needs. Ultimately, my self-centeredness damaged my reputation and, in the end, led to loneliness.

Self-inflicted wounds are sometimes the hardest to heal. They require full acceptance, taking accountability, self-forgiveness, self-awareness, grace, and a conscious vow to never repeat the behavior again.

Lord God, forgive me. Because I have transgressed against my neighbor, and I have coveted what does not belong to me. I am lost. I am broken. I need to be found and put back together again. Help me, Oh Lord! In the name of Jesus. Amen.

I inadvertently made relationships challenging because I refused to relinquish pride. Pride made it hard for me to love myself, and even harder for others to love me. Pride shielded my ears and my heart. It slithered its way into my relationships and evoked an arrogant sense of entitlement. I became the porter of narcissism. They say, "Pride comes before the fall". Well, on this journey, I fell and failed repeatedly.

After experiencing so many cuts and bruises, I realized that I needed to surrender pride; I recognized the harm in it. Releasing pride gave rise to empathy for others, allowed me to foster compassion, and develop deeper connections. I became less conceited and full of humility, which allowed me to live more gracefully.

Some people have no intention of growing beyond the life they have, and that's okay. But to elevate, sometimes you must separate. Learn to love people from a distance and surround yourself with people who add value and purpose to your life. People who motivate you and who inspire you to walk and live in your purpose.

"Marry a man who loves you more than you love him" is what I used to say. I used to brag about how much my man loved me because he provided me with material things, but in my ignorance, I failed to realize that my marriage lacked substance. It lacked peace, joy, kindness, understanding, and genuine love, but most importantly, it lacked God. I erred because I was too busy revering myself, while I should have been revering God. "Marry a man who loves God more than he loves you" is what I should have been saying.

I began to set my mind on greater things. I replaced the man who inflicted pain with a godly man. I figured that if I could create such a pleasant man in my imagination, then perhaps I could recondition my mind to learn how to love a godly man. At first, satanic thoughts filled my mind and made me believe that I was not worthy of a "good, godly man," but with healing came a new mindset, greater expectations, and a self-confidence that I never had.

Marrying a godly man can offer benefits such as a strong foundation of commitment, unwavering love, spiritual growth, a sense of security, leadership based on Christian principles, a supportive partner who prioritizes family values, and a commitment to working through challenges together, guided by faith. A man whose cup is full of oil and can pour into me everything that I need, and I can pour back into him. I deserve this type of man, and I became intentional about consecrating myself in anticipation and in preparation for receiving him.

I heard the spirit of the Lord say, "I am adorning you." To be adorned means to be decorated, beautified, and embellished with elegant additions. To be enhanced by making something or someone more attractive. Thank you, Father, for spending time on me. I can't wait for him to behold my beauty. Behold, He makes all things new. Rev 21:5.

"When I was a child, I spoke as a child, I understood as a child, I thought as a child; but when I became a man, I put away childish things." 1 Corinthians 13:11.

A person attracts who and what they are. A broken person attracts a broken person, and a healed person attracts a healed person. This is why it is important to embrace transformation and change, because it is necessary in life and for progression. When you realize that the person you were once attracted to no longer exists because they have made a conscious decision to heal, it then becomes your decision to grow alongside them and change for the better. But if you choose not to grow, then gracefully step aside for the next person to bask in healed territory.

Reflection Questions: **What things from your past can you take accountability for? Be specific. What would you say to a person in an abusive relationship? Or what would you say to yourself if you are or was that person?**

LIKE FRESH OIL

Healing was understanding that love is letting go.

Love is Letting Go

"Truly, your God is God of gods, and Lord of kings, and a revealer of mysteries."
Daniel 2:47

I had entered the gates, and at the entrance was a golden stand. Jr. laid on this stand. Although his body was lifeless, his appearance was lifelike and radiant. On his left ankle was a bracelet like a dog tag. This bracelet was made of a bright, golden-yellow precious metal. It was the most beautiful, genuine gold I had ever seen; it felt heavy in my hand. Engraved in the tag was a symbol of a lion. Every detail had been delicately carved with precision. I knew exactly where I was; I had entered The Kingdom, the dwelling place of the Lion of Judah.

The hidden mysteries of God. Could it be possible that our stillborn babies are blessed with special privileges and accommodations, allowing their bodies to be captured from the earth and taken to the Father? Is my son's body not in that grave that I saw them bury him in? Could Christ have sent his angels to collect our innocent babies because their flesh is sinless? Could this be God's will?

To the left was a golden vault, massive in structure, with hundreds of drawers. In each compartment were bodies of babies who rested in sacred tombs. Jr's body is no longer in that grave. The creator Himself is preserving his body.

To the right was a platform. The floor was made of crystals and clear glass. On this platform sat a white couch. I was accompanied in spirit by my younger brother and my mother, whom I couldn't see but only felt her spirit. It was like a visitation room. As we sat on the couch waiting, Jr. appeared in my presence. He looked to be about four years old.

"Hi, Mommy," he said as he jumped into my lap. I held my son; I kissed his lips. I never wanted to let him go.

"Hi, baby. How are you doing?" I asked.

He replied, "Good." He was strong, playful, and energetic.

"I love you, son," I said. "I love you too, Mommy," he responded.

"Jr., do you want to come back to earth with me?" I asked.

He replied, "No, I'm okay here." He jumped into my brothers' arms, and they began to horseplay together.

I knew I had entered a realm elevated above the world, so I propped myself up to look behind the couch. I was amazed as I looked down at the Earth.

When I turned around, Jr. was jumping, skipping, and kicking a pebble across the ground. He had run away a bit too far for my liking. My motherly instinct was to yell, "Come back, you're going too far!" But the spirit instantly made me realize that I couldn't tell him that because there are no limits or boundaries in The Kingdom, no restrictions; therefore, he was free to go as far as he chose.

"Mommy, do you want to meet my brothers and sisters?" he asked.

In confusion, I replied, "Yes." He went away for a moment, and when he returned, he came back with four other children. Two older children, one boy and one girl, and two younger children, one boy and one girl. Jr. stood next to me. All five of my children stood before me, my children, and those who were yet to come. I marveled in awe because God, in his faithfulness, had shown me my children, and my children that I had aborted in college, that they are being kept, and they are alright.

Father God had favored me so greatly that He gave me the opportunity to visit Heaven and pay a visit to my children. Oh, how good and how merciful my God has been to me. I will carry His goodness in my heart forever. I will walk this journey, always knowing that God is real. Heaven is real.

To the mother who lost a baby at birth. Don't you worry because God has constructed a plan. A plan that is beyond our imagination; a plan so marvelous that it could not be written. Stand firm and trust by faith in the hidden mysteries of God. Our Creator, in due season, will put everything back together in its perfect and proper place.

To the mother who gave a baby up for abortion, don't beat yourself up about your decision any longer because God has constructed a plan for you, too. With grace and faith, trust that your baby is alright. In your imperfections, God is perfect. They are patiently waiting for you to be their mother in The Kingdom.

To any mother who has lost a child, don't worry. I know that your heart is heavy, and this burden may seem too hard to bear, but your child has entered a realm that is more profoundly majestic and perfect than our minds can ever imagine. A polished place that was designed by the God of gods. Your child has entered into a rest that we have never experienced; a place of joy and everlasting life. They are in glory and dwelling in the presence of God.

They are okay, I promise.

Oh, mother, do not fret, "Let not your heart be troubled; you believe in God, believe also in Me. In My Father's house are many mansions; if it were not so, I would have told you. I go to prepare a place for you. And if I go and prepare a place for you, I will come again and receive you to Myself; that where I am, there you may be also." (John 14-1-3)

Oh, Mother,

"Be still and know that I am God." (Psalm 46:10)

Dear "Bro",

I loved you before you were born. Before I ever laid eyes on you, I carried you in my soul. I petitioned to The Queen for you. As tears, snot, and saliva drooled down my face, I desperately interceded for your existence because I did not want death to meet you. I begged for the opportunity to love you, to hold you, to live in your presence. I vowed to cherish you unconditionally. I yearned to make you my priority. "I will love my baby brother or my baby sister! I will take care of it. I promise. It'll be my baby! Please, don't get rid of it!" I pleaded. When The Queen finally conceded to my intercession, I proclaimed that you would have life, and life more abundantly.

Even before your birth, my spirit knew you. I understood that the world would be a better place with you in it, that your spirit would thrive and cultivate purpose. When I met you, you were perfect, and you were mine; it didn't matter that I was seven years old. You stayed by my side. I was there when you took your first step, and when you fell down and bashed your head on the coffee table. I held you in my arms as blood gushed from your head, trying to keep you awake in the back seat as Mama drove you to the hospital. I held your hands with tears streaming down my face as the doctor sewed stitches in your forehead. I remember your screams, and I remember wiping your tears.

As we grew up, I made a conscious effort to be a positive role model for you. I wasn't perfect and didn't always make the right decisions, but for you, I strived to be an outlet, a haven that you could always come to in times of weakness or discomfort. As I watched you grow into a man, it happened so quickly, but time had to get us here. I watched you foster greatness. You were never a problem and never got into mischievous behaviors. You chose a good crowd. You've never been arrested and don't have a record. You love the Lord. I was proud as I watched you transform into everything a good woman deserves. Your heart is pure. God created you with cause.

When He created you, He took His time to put into you everything that He wanted you to have. You are perfectly made, with an extra dose of kindness. When God made you, I believe He had me in mind because He knew that I needed you. He knew that within you was a light that would illuminate my darkness, a light that I so desperately needed. A healing light. I can remember when I left for college, I begged my boyfriend to look after you. "Please look after my lil brother. Make sure he stays safe. Take care of him." He agreed to get you as much as he could. I was thankful because I worried about you when I was away.

It didn't matter how much we fought or argued. It didn't matter that you never stopped talking or had the energy of a Tasmanian devil; all that mattered was that you were here with me.

I had asked God why He allowed your spirit to accompany me to visit Jr. in Heaven. "Lord, what about his presence was needed?" I asked.

The spirit responded, "Because he's your soul mate. Your souls are intertwined. This is how I made it."

"Thank you, Lord, for that revelation." Because it made perfect sense to me.

This made sense because Jr. knew you; he recognized you. Your spirits had once dwelled together in The Kingdom. When he saw you, he embraced you like no stranger.

Your existence is relevant. I need you to walk this earth knowing that God's got you. You're locked in, and no worldly choice can diminish what God placed in you. You are set apart; you are not like them. You are great and filled with profound thoughts and concepts that the world sometimes won't understand. A simple-minded man will not comprehend the language that you speak because your language is elevated and grace-filled. God personally gave you a portion of Himself and packed it away so deeply inside of you that sometimes it's hard for you even to see it. But, Bro, rest easy. Even when you can't feel His presence, know that He will never leave you or forsake you. He will be there even until the end of the world. Walk boldly and with your head held high, trusting that every wound and all the pain will indeed breed a purpose.

I love you from the depths of my soul. I am proud to call you my brother and my friend.

I am my brother's keeper.

Reflection Questions: Do you give yourself grace? What are the ways that you know God has given you grace?

LOVE IS LETTING GO

Healing was walking into my purpose.

Walking in Purpose

*"Your purpose is not the thing you do.
Your purpose is the thing that happens in others
when you do what you do."*
Dr. Caroline Leaf

Born and raised in an urban St. Louis area, I witnessed and endured a great deal of hardship and adversity. Trauma was that thing that just came with the territory. I have always known that whatever path I chose, I wanted it to be grounded in helping people in my community. I was unsure what path God had ordained for me, but life's ebbs and flows had gotten me to a point where I recognized my calling. My life had begun to make sense. For many years, I questioned, "God, why have you allowed me to endure so much? What is the purpose of it all?"

I was raised in a Christian denomination. I had always trusted in God. I attended church and became acclimated to this lifestyle as a young child. It worked for me. It gave me hope and a sense of fulfillment that I don't believe I could have found in believing in anything else.

When I was twelve years old, my mother took me to a church. I remember a middle-aged woman praying with me, and in that prayer, she mentioned that she had received a word from God concerning my life. She said, "I see a level of education that will take you higher." Those words had stuck in my heart and mind for over twenty-two years. I clung to her words, trusting that one day God would make sense of it. He did.

We go through things in life to help the next person and to let our story be a beacon of hope for a neighbor. When I decided to walk in my purpose, I realized that a career in counseling was what God had ordained for me. Pursuing a career as a professional counselor allowed me to turn all the ugly things that I had endured into something beautiful. What greater way than to use this level of education to elevate myself and take my community with me along the way?

I obtained a bachelor's degree in the field of criminal and juvenile justice. Soon afterward, I landed a job in the field of behavioral health. I thrived in this position and richly enjoyed every moment of the job. It was a pleasure to be a part of the healing process for so many young boys and girls. Not only did I enjoy it, but I was good at it.

Some years later, I desired to return to school, earning a master's degree in legal studies and a paralegal certificate. I desired to attend law school one day. I wanted to be the change I wanted to see. I went on to work for multiple law firms as a paralegal and legal assistant. Although I gained a great deal of knowledge,

I never felt fulfillment in that line of work. I have held several positions, but none compared to the contentment I felt when working directly with people in behavioral health.

"The right doors won't open for you until you become the version of yourself that is supposed to walk through them." Mental health, mental illness, depression, suicide, rage, self-esteem, and trauma in the black community are taboo topics that are often swept under the rug. Many people in my community reject therapy because it is translated as "weak." Historically speaking, blacks are more likely to go without emotional support, emotional safety, non-biased medical care, and non-biased mental health support.

Few people realize the benefits of participating in counseling. Counseling can be an outlet to release burdens. It can help you process trauma through self-discovery and explore who you are beyond your roles in the family, community, or at work. Therapy can aid in navigating relationships with friends and family, and it can increase resilience while helping to build a healthier sense of self. Counselors will teach you how to set boundaries and demonstrate vulnerability in a healthy way. I know from personal experience that therapy is a safe and supportive space. When you do the work, you'll receive a divine healing, and you'll be compelled to walk into your purpose.

Choosing therapy was the best decision of my life. If you struggle with deciding if therapy is for you, here are some ways to overcome these challenges.

- Educate yourself. Discover various types of therapy and their potential benefits for you. Talk to your primary care physician; they can provide referrals and discuss options.

- Do your research. Look for therapists in your area who specialize in the issues you are facing, and be sure to read their reviews. Online therapy is an option; explore platforms that offer telehealth services for added flexibility.

- Reach out to your insurance provider if your financial situation is a concern. Check to see if your plan offers mental health services and find out ahead of time what your copay may be.

- Talk to a trusted friend or family member; their support can be invaluable in helping you overcome your insecurities.

A good therapist? See, a good therapist will break you down. But once you form trust, you have to believe that they will build you back up again.

Reflection Questions: **If you were to walk into your full purpose, what would it look like? What steps could you take to fulfill your purpose?**

_____
_____
_____
_____
_____
_____
_____
_____
_____
_____
_____
_____
_____
_____
_____
_____
_____
_____
_____
_____
_____

LIKE FRESH OIL

Healing was refusing to harbor secrets any longer.

Harboring Secrets

Luke 8:17
"For there is nothing hidden that will not be disclosed, and nothing concealed that will not be known or brought out into the open."

Darkness and light cannot dwell together.

As hard as I try, it's always nearly impossible for me to accurately express with words the mental crisis I had after Cravis and his wife verbally attacked me in the middle of the family reunion. When Cravis came around, I never really looked his way. This was my survival mechanism and how I coped with his presence over the years because Cravis had never apologized, admitted, or spoken about what he did to me. I knew what he was capable of. I kept my distance from him, and I taught my daughter to do the same. As far as I was concerned, he didn't have any reason to look my way or to say my name.

It was evident that he had not been honest with his wife concerning his past behaviors and our history, because if he had, she would have understood the distance I had placed between us. Instead of being woman enough to come to have a conversation with me regarding her sentiments, she chose to lash out at me in ignorance. She disturbed the peace at our reunion and completely embarrassed herself through harsh allegations, threatening gestures, and blatant disrespect. I was embarrassed for her because, "Honey, if you only knew the truth about who your husband really is, you would not be standing here in my face, talking foolishness to me." That is what I wanted to say.

But the spirit silenced me. In the midst of this unforeseen chaos, I was forced to remain silent. It was like God had zipped my lips and bridled my tongue. I couldn't understand why I couldn't say what I wanted. The words were right there in my mind, on the tip of my tongue, yet I couldn't push the words out. However, the words that I said were graceful.

It wasn't until after the drama ended that God revealed to me why I couldn't say what I wanted to say. As I looked around the room, no one of significance was there to witness this attack, not one of my uncles. Most of the males who would have intervened had either already left for the evening or were outside congregating. If I had let her pull out of me the reaction that she wanted or said what was on my mind regarding Cravis and his character, he and his wife would have physically attacked me, and there would have been no male in the room to protect me. God saw this and silenced me; He saw the outcome of what could have been. In that moment, my Heavenly Father was my protector.

The red that I saw scared me, and instantly, my mental health declined.

RAGE!

Thoughts of murder!

How dare he even speak my name?

How dare she falsely accuse me of acts that never took place?

I kept silent to preserve the peace all this time, and you come in here starting shit with me after all this time? You weak coward. You lack integrity, and I am afraid for that woman and her daughter, I thought.

I cried often. I was sleep-deprived. I was heavy with the need for revenge. I was broken. Cravis and Keith together had won. They had set a goal to break me, and in that moment, the goal was accomplished because I was defeated. I tried every day to keep it together for the sake of my daughter, but I failed. Everything that I had carried for so long came to a head. It was like I was in hell. Together, they had ignited a fire in my mind, and I desperately needed someone to come to my rescue. Thank God for Jesus. Thank God for my therapist.

Family skeletons took a toll on my mental health and happiness. For years, I didn't tell anyone about my abuse. No one knew the specifics or how long it lasted; my closest friend knew only vague details, but no one truly understood the torment that I had endured for so long. A series of crises pushed my harboring beyond my limit. I recognized that I was not only hiding my own secrets, but I was harboring my abuser's secrets, too. My silence had protected them, but when Cravis and his wife decided to verbally attack me at the family reunion, I had reached my peak, and I refused to preserve his "good man" image another day at the expense of my own mental health.

I became full of rage. I was angry with the world and ready to fight anyone who didn't consider my feelings. I unintentionally sabotaged relationships because I was so broken, mean, and unattractive. I had internalized this trauma so deeply that it made me physically sick. My body suffered from aches and pains due to stress. I suffered from migraines because my mind was always boggled with dysfunction. The day that I spoke up was the day that I became free, because I realized that the spirit of God cannot dwell in the same place as these harbored secrets, skeletons, and demons. I was thirty-four years old when I finally told my mother the whole truth about Cravis; how long the molestation occurred and the threats that silenced me. I also told her about Keith and how he had forced me to become his victim of child pornography.

Too often, families and friends keep secrets to protect others from historical or current information they feel will be too painful or embarrassing to disclose. Some of them simply lack integrity. The problem is that secrets come with a cost; they burden us mentally, emotionally, and spiritually. They preoccupy us and deteriorate our healthy minds; it spreads like cancer. Secrets jeopardize relationships across generations, and they are detrimental to humanity because they are rooted in lies, manipulation, and deception, all of which are not of God. After thirty years, I decided that I no longer wanted to harbor these secrets, and I became adamant about separating myself from people who did not share the same values.

That night, I dreamed that I was sitting on a mountain, and all around me were cascading waterfalls with vibrant colors that illuminated the rocks and rainbows shining from the sky. The atmosphere was serene, and my spirit was harmonious with the spirit of God. These waterfalls represented the process of letting go of negative thoughts. The water was a symbol of the spirit, and the waterfalls acted as a spiritual cleanse that removed negative energy from my mind, body, and soul. The rainbows were a representation of God's promise. God had once again shown me, in His faithfulness, miraculous signs and wonders.

Reflection Questions: In what areas are you weak? How could you be made stronger?

LIKE FRESH OIL

Healing was surrendering myself to the mercy of God.

Surrendering to the Mercy of God

¹⁰ That at the name of Jesus every knee should bow, in heaven and on earth and under the earth, ¹¹ and every tongue acknowledge that Jesus Christ is Lord, to the glory of God the Father.
Philippians 2:10-11 NIV

I was nineteen years old when God first spoke to me. I was headed to class that early afternoon when He met me in my car. I can still remember the voice, so soft yet clear and concise. He made me a promise, saying, "I will restore what you have lost."

Days later, it was the same scenario. God met me at the exact same time and place. He said, "Your faith has made you whole." None of this made sense to me because I couldn't recall anything that I had lost, and I didn't know what faithful actions I had displayed. Amid my confusion, He had threaded these words into my heart. God, in His infinite glory, had met me twice regarding two different topics that I had no idea the meaning behind them. I trusted that one day, he would reveal the purpose of speaking those words to me.

The term obsessive decluttering differs from simply being tidy in that it manifests in a more extreme manner. A person experiencing decluttering believes that certain objects negatively affect their life and, therefore, must be discarded, even if the objects are still in use or could be of good use. Those who experience this face the issue of being obsessed with cleaning the house, and they will not feel better until it is done. This is me. I wear it like a badge of honor because when people need help cleaning, organizing, or decluttering, they know who to call. I am not exaggerating when I say that throwing things in the trash is second nature for me. Decluttering makes me feel less stressed and reduces anxiety; it improves my focus and concentration. More importantly, it helps me feel a sense of accomplishment and control over my surroundings.

I had treated myself to a date night, and these date nights had become a self-care non-negotiable because I enjoyed the time spent with just me and God. I ordered my food and began reading the book of Proverbs, making an intentional effort to read my Bible more. During reflection, I thought about my past, the need to go home and clean my house, and my daughter; it was just a series of wandering thoughts. Then, the spirit spoke to me crystal clear, "Just as easy as it is for you to throw things away, it should be just as easy for you to get rid of the things that you have been holding inside." In that moment, God had given me a spiritual revelation. In His infinite wisdom, He had linked my physical and spiritual attributes together to help me understand the simplicity of releasing the filth I had been harboring internally for decades.

LIKE FRESH OIL

"Heavenly Father, in the mighty and majestic name of Jesus, Lord, I come before your throne humbly asking permission to lay at your feet. Lord, I surrender myself to you. You are The King, my Savior, and my Redeemer. Lord, I come to you first, asking for your forgiveness for the trespasses I have committed against your will. Deliver me from excuses and lies. These lies have so deeply cultivated my mind and punctured my heart that I became blind to your will and my purpose. Release the bounds of sin. Oh Lord, I am reminded at this moment that I have been empowered to live a life of holiness, a life full of peace and serenity. Lord, pour into me like fresh oil, a constant spirit of reverence and a spirit of honor. As I begin to seek you even more diligently, please give me a spirit of respect so profound that a holy fear prevents me from turning away from you. Give me a desire for moral purity that I will never compromise again. Lord, give me a heart to maintain forgiveness for the pain that my enemies inflicted on me."

As I prayed this prayer, I saw two men, tall in stature, one on my right and one on my left. They held me on both sides with one hand on my torso and the other on my back; it was as if they were waiting for something to happen. The man on the right fed me every word to say, "Lord, I lay it all at your feet. Hurt, pain, lies, molestation, rape, deceit, sadness, worry, struggles, anxiety, depression, suicide, devastation, sickness, cancer, an ill mind, rage, envy, doubt, low self-esteem, manipulation, anger, isolation, revenge, guilt, loneliness, hopelessness, hate, helplessness, death, murder, regret, resentment, jealousy, hypervigilance, generational curses, trauma, fear, violence, addiction, drunkenness, drugs, strife". He said, "Now open your eyes." When I opened my eyes, he asked, "What do you see?"

I responded, "A pile of garbage." There, laid at the feet of God, was a huge pile of black dump.

God ordered me to "bring him here." I knew exactly who He wanted. When we returned, Keith stood trembling before the Lord, knowing that his punishment would be great and much deserved. God, with authority, demanded that Keith "bow down before me." All of this was happening inside my prayer. The harder I prayed, the deeper Keith bowed. It was like my words were sculpting his body, and by the time I had finished praying, Keith's body was crippled, and his back was drastically hunched over; he kneeled before the Lord, bowed at His feet, like a footstool. His punishment was to stay there for eternity.

The man on the right side whispered in my ear, "Now throw it away." Instantly, vomit came from the pit of my stomach; an incredible amount of it. I gasped for air in between each gag. This is what those men were waiting for. I was literally purging all the filth that I had stored away in my soul in storage bags. As I watched the mess fall into the toilet, I declared my greatness and my healing. The more I regurgitated, the more those men spoke life into me. I wept in prayer and praise. It was as if the spirit was pouring back into me the portion that was spewing out, like fresh oil.

Reflection: Write a letter to God.

Healing was learning how to nurture myself.

Nurturing

You love yourself differently when you learn how much you truly mean to God.

Everyone heals differently because everyone's wounds need a different kind of nurturing. While I may need stitches, you may need glue. While it took me ten months to heal from abuse, it may take you six. There is no set time for healing. For some people, healing can take a lifetime. But if we are intentional about nurturing our wounds, healing will manifest; everything is in God's time.

Physical Health:

- How many hours of sleep do you typically get per night?
- How often do you engage in physical activity?
- Do you regularly schedule medical checkups?

Mental Wellbeing:

- How often do you practice relaxation techniques, such as meditation or deep breathing?
- How would you rate your current level of stress?
- Do you have healthy coping strategies for dealing with stress?
- How often do you take time for hobbies or activities you enjoy?

Social Connections:

- Do you feel comfortable reaching out for support when you need it?
- How satisfied are you with your social life?
- Do you feel comfortable saying "no" to things that compromise your mental well-being?

Self-Reflection:

- What are your biggest challenges related to self-care?
- What self-care practices would you like to incorporate more in your life?
- What are your biggest sources of stress, and how do you manage them?

These were a set of questions on a questionnaire that was given to me at the beginning of my healing journey. I recall feeling annoyed and uncomfortable while taking this questionnaire, because I couldn't understand half the questions and had never given these topics much thought.

I can remember how vague and simple I answered her questions. "What are some ways that you nurture yourself?" she asked. I responded, "Well, I get my nails done every two weeks. I take myself to dinner or buy myself something nice when I can afford it. I take showers every day and make sure to wash my hair every week. I want to exercise and eat right. I don't always have time to do what I want, but I do what I can when I can."

She looked at me, shook her head, and said, "You have no idea what it means to nurture yourself."

"What about self-esteem? What does it mean to you?" she asked.

"Hmm, self-esteem is feeling good about myself, I guess," I vaguely responded.

"Okay," she replied. Tears welled up in the ducts of my eyes because I knew that I lacked self-esteem and had no clue what it meant to nurture myself. I was embarrassed because I knew she could see right through me, that I didn't possess an ounce of self-esteem, and that I had lacked proper nurturing throughout my life.

The greatest lesson in learning how to nurture myself was how to grow my self-esteem. Once I could perceive myself as worthy, desirable, and beautiful, then I could treat myself as such. Most of us are mentally conditioned to use negative attacks to improve ourselves, or we'll use condemnation to get ourselves back on the right track. We'll put the negative before the positive and expect a positive outcome. But is this a distorted way of thinking or an ill mind? I began to categorize my thoughts as either an "ill mind" or a "healthy mind."

First, it is important to understand that there is a difference between an "ill mind" and a "mental illness." An "ill mind" can be placed on a spectrum to describe a negative mental state. It is a term that describes a state of temporary decline in mental well-being. An "ill mind" could include poor decision-making, feeling entitled, feeling overwhelmed, anxiety, or acting impulsively. "Mental illness" refers to a diagnosable medical condition that significantly disrupts a person's thinking, feelings, and behaviors. So, I am not referring to a mental illness but an ill mind.

A "healthy mind" is a state of well-being that encompasses your emotional, psychological, and social health. It allows us to cope with stress, adapt to change, make good choices, and do away with judgment. A critical component of self-esteem is letting go of judgment. Giving up judgment allows us to make decisions about what to include and exclude from our lives.

Let's take a deeper dive for a better understanding. If we were to list all the bad things in the world, it would look something like this: Stealing, murder, molestation, rape, drugs, addiction, suicide, gossip, lies, poverty, war, cancer, disease, human trafficking, inequality, racism, violence, natural disasters, kidnapping, hunger, homelessness, terrorism, sexism, etc.

Now, if we were to list all the things that we don't like about ourselves, it would sound something like this: My eyes are too big. My feet are ugly. My hips are not curvy. My butt is flat. My skin is rough. My nose is too wide. I'm too short. My hair is thin. My lips are big. My teeth are crooked. My skin has dark spots. I look fat. I am skinny. My muscles are not big enough. I can't do this, and I can't do that, and so on.

When we subject ourselves to negative judgments, we ignorantly place ourselves in the same category as all the other bad things in the world.

The habit of judgment is built into our inherited survival strategies. But when we strive to set our minds on greater things, we dismantle Satan's mission and uphold a standard that transforms us into who God predestined us to be from the beginning. Self-judgment is not of God because Christ has already declared who we are. If we were made in His image and His likeness, then who are we to call ourselves anything less than perfect?

Learning how to nurture myself was learning how to accept my flaws. She said, "I challenge you to go to the store, pick out the sexiest swimsuit you can find, put it on, stand in front of the mirror, look at yourself, and compliment every part of your body for 30 minutes straight, every day." At first, this was challenging and seemed silly, but with practice, it got easy. Becoming intentional about complimenting myself boosted my confidence and self-image. I began to love myself.

"Excuses are monuments of nothingness; they build bridges to nowhere, and those who use these tools of incompetence seldom become anything but nothing at all." I began using this quote to hold myself accountable. I started making myself a priority, minus excuses.

She said, "You should stop making excuses and carve out time for yourself just like you make time for everything and everybody else. You should start setting money aside every week to do something just for you. Create a list of self-care non-negotiables. Create a list of places you want to visit and things you want to do, and be intentional about accomplishing those goals. Don't wait around for anybody. Do what you enjoy."

Healing requires intentionality, strategic planning, and a close examination of every area of our lives. Healing mentally requires acknowledging and expressing your feelings. Emotional healing is the process of accepting and working through difficult emotions and experiences. Healing spiritually requires a great deal of prayer, sacrifice, reading the Word of God, and repentance.

Healing socially is embracing the support of a community. Healing physically requires eating well, getting adequate rest, and maintaining good hygiene and daily muscle movement.

When I reflect on everything God is to me, it inspires me to be that to myself more and more. God is faithful to me; therefore, I will be faithful to myself. God loves me; therefore, I will love myself. God is graceful; therefore, I will give myself grace. God is kind; therefore, I will show kindness to myself. My body is the temple of the Holy Spirit, so taking care of it is creating an immaculate space for the Spirit of God to dwell.

Childhood sexual trauma had a way of restricting my growth and development. It has been proven through research that childhood sexual abuse can be directly associated with a plethora of neuropsychological deficiencies related to PTSD, communicative dysfunctions, and cognitive development. There were times that I felt like an eight-year-old child inside a thirty-year-old body. My abuse hindered my mental capability to thrive like a typical non-abused woman. I sometimes noticed that when my voice sounded like a child's, it was because I was responding to someone older than me. I noticed that I would sometimes sit like a child. I lacked femininity and the poise that I often saw in other grown women my age. They appeared to be so in touch with their femininity, while I felt trapped in a childlike state of mind.

The person I was then is not the person I am today. I became intentional about putting a little extra sway in my hips when I walked and a little base in my voice when I talked. Instead of just grabbing the first thing I saw from the clothes hamper, I began taking my time to pick out my clothes. I started a skincare routine and selected fragrances that reminded me of scents I had smelled on other women. I started wearing my hair in styles that no longer made me look like a little girl, but even if

I chose a ponytail, a splash of foundation, a touch of eyeliner, and a pop of mascara always accompanied. I refused to be stuck inside that little girl anymore.

I ate a variety of vegetables and fruits, as well as berries, and took a whole food fortified multivitamin every day to help keep my mind regulated. I stopped eating red meat and pork periodically and only consumed fish and chicken to increase my protein and fatty acid intake.

A Soror introduced me to breathwork. I attended a breathwork class and was taught how to breathe. Breathwork refers to a set of techniques that involve intentional and conscious control of breathing patterns. It aims to improve physical, mental, and emotional well-being by regulating the flow of air into and out of the body. Deep, diaphragmatic breathing activities help reduce stress hormones. Breathwork can also help calm the mind and body, leading to improved sleep patterns. There is a profound biblical symbolism associated with breath and spiritual life. Genesis 2:7 says, "Then the Lord God formed the man from the dust of the ground and breathed into his nostrils the breath of life, and the man became a living being." Every breath that we take is a gift from the living God. Psalms 150:6 advises, "Let everything that has breath praise the Lord." Christ Himself exemplified breathing in the book of John when He breathed on the disciples and said to them, "Receive the Holy Spirit."

I was in a car accident on the 4th of July; a car struck us from behind at a high speed. I instantly felt pain in my back from the impact. I had a spinal cord injury that has caused me to have chronic pain in my neck, back, and shoulders. Along with regularly scheduled massages and frequent visits to the chiropractor, I resorted to using vibration as a natural and holistic healing approach. The power of vibration and frequencies promotes physical and emotional healing by stimulating the nervous system, reducing pain, tension, and muscle spasm, and promoting relaxation.

I began drinking a gallon of water every day, after consuming a cup of mushroom coffee. These mushrooms are considered superfoods. Drinking mushroom coffee daily offered benefits like a smoother, more sustained energy boost, improved my focus, and helped with stress management and cognitive function.

I no longer drink or fornicate. God caused many people to fall off; therefore, I no longer curse because those who pushed me to anger no longer exist in my circle. Am I perfect? No. Do I have it all figured out? Absolutely not. But I am intentional about not turning back. I can't turn back because I've come too far.

People do change, and people do grow out of immature behaviors. People can adapt to new mindsets. People draw closer to God, and it changes their outlook on life. The same person you knew two weeks ago could have experienced something that turned their whole life around; it is possible. So, stop judging people just because you don't know that version of them. Enjoy the version you had and get to know the new one, too; if not, keep your opinions to yourself and move on, because no one cares about who you used to be or what you used to do. "Therefore, if any man be in Christ, he is a new creature; old things are passed away, behold all things have become new." 2 Corinthians 5:17

Reflection Question: What are your self-care non-negotiables? If you don't have any, use the lines below to create some.

LIKE FRESH OIL

Healing was not abandoning wisdom.

Not Abandoning Wisdom

Healing requires repositioning your heart's posture.

The person I was is not the person I am today because, in my imagination, I had become like King Solomon. Solomon was wiser than anyone because he prayed for wisdom, aligning his heart toward heaven and giving priority to God over the world's ways.

When I began my healing journey, I also prayed for God's wisdom and understanding. My past traumas had stripped away every bit of my femininity. I did not know how to bask in feminine energy, and I shrank in the presence of other women. When I began to read the book of Proverbs, the words started to transform me, and my head was lifted as I listened to God refer to wisdom as "she."

Proverbs 4:1-9 *Christian Standard Bible*

4 Listen, sons, to a father's discipline,
and pay attention so that you may gain understanding,
² for I am giving you good instruction.
Don't abandon my teaching.
³ When I was a son with my father,
tender and precious to my mother,
⁴ he taught me and said,
"Your heart must hold on to my words.
Keep my commands and live.
⁵ Get wisdom, get understanding;
don't forget or turn away from the words from my mouth.
⁶ Don't abandon wisdom, and she will watch over you;
love her, and she will guard you.
⁷ Wisdom is supreme—so get wisdom.
And whatever else you get, get understanding.
⁸ Cherish her, and she will exalt you;
if you embrace her, she will honor you.
⁹ She will place a garland of favor on your head;
she will give you a crown of beauty."

Not abandoning wisdom allowed me to cultivate the qualities associated with feminine energy, such as the ability to tap into my intuition and enhance my creativity. Wisdom was knowing when to speak and when to keep silent. Healing was putting it into action. Sometimes, the wisest thing is to say nothing. This required humility, rather than weighing in on every topic or sharing an opinion about things I hadn't done much research on. Wisdom taught me how to remain silent rather than opening my mouth and how to listen for understanding. Wisdom is from God and is to be used and stewarded for His benefit. When we forget the source, we risk losing it all.

So, how do I know if I lack wisdom? You lack wisdom when you don't have the desire to grow or learn anything new. You care more about the moment rather than the outcome. You are impulsive and impromptu. You live in past mistakes. You are impressed by what the world has to offer.

Wisdom came to me because I desired it. With wisdom, I now possess a discerning spirit and the ability to distinguish between good and evil.

"Lord, give me wisdom that surpasses all understanding. Seal my lips and guard my tongue. Let your Word restrict me when needed. Give me wisdom that I won't choose a path of destruction and guide my feet so that I may enter your presence. Continue to mold me into who You want me to be. Lord, clear my mind of clouds and rid me of distress. Speak to my heart, Lord. In the name of Jesus. Amen."

Practicing celibacy is sometimes challenging; it is probably the most challenging thing I've ever done. Because my flesh and my spirit battled often. Did I ever desire sex? Yes. But my desire to master self-control outweighed my urgency, and my will to sacrifice for Christ overpowered my fleshly wants. Logical reasoning (wisdom) suggested that if you prayed and asked God to stay in your presence, why would you offend Him and indulge in such perverse acts in His presence? I didn't want to disrespect Him in that way. Wisdom asked, "Would you do this while your parents watched?" Absolutely not, because not only would it be disrespectful, but it would be immoral. I considered God's feelings. I began to be more mindful of my actions and more inquisitive about how God saw me. "What does God see when He looks at me?" I asked myself. With this new perspective, participating in such acts would be shameful, and I didn't want to grieve the Holy Spirit. God gave me the stamina to endure this fast, and in times of struggle, I placed myself at the Cross, remembering how much Jesus suffered for me. How much pain and discomfort He endured for little ol' me. Who am I to complain?

I went back to my first love. God became my husbandman, and I made love to Him daily.

If you want to learn what truly binds you, try fasting from it. Isaiah 58:6 states, "Is this not the fast that I choose: to loosen the bonds of wickedness, to untie the cords of the yoke, to break free the oppressed, and to break every yoke?" Healing is understanding a true fast. One that goes beyond fasting from food, yet focuses on acts of righteousness. True fasting goes beyond physical abstention. It's not about looking good on the outside or feeling a sense of accomplishment, but it's about inner transformation and a commitment to living in accordance with God's will, God's Word, and God's purpose for your life.

Fast, pray, and heal!

Healing is more than the mending of brokenness—it is the unveiling of God's love in our lives. Every wound healed, every scar turned into a testimony reflects His mercy.

When we are restored, we are not just made whole; we are reminded of the majesty of the One who heals. His dignity is displayed in His patience with us, His love that never fails, and His power that transforms pain into purpose. To recognize the dignity of the Lord through healing is to see Him as the Great Physician of body, mind, and spirit. It is to acknowledge that only in His presence can we truly find peace, restoration, and eternal hope. Our healing is not just about us—it is about glorifying the One who lifts us from despair and sets us on solid ground.

God showed me miracle after miracle and poured down blessing after blessing, bestowing an insurmountable amount of grace and favor upon me. Then, The Queen told me that my heart wasn't right. I was so bothered in my mind, shaken by her words. I did some soul-searching, but I couldn't find the relevance of her words. I questioned my character. I doubted whether I was good enough or if I was living life right. I knew that I was a good person. I displayed acts of kindness. I did charitable deeds. I forgave. I would go above and beyond for the people I love, and I do the same for strangers. I show love. I give grace. So, what about my heart wasn't right? I could not figure it out. I tossed and turned all night. My psyche was disturbed, and my spirit was distraught. Was there something about myself that I didn't know or something that I didn't recognize? "What does God see when he looks into my heart?" I questioned.

"A wise man knows he knows nothing." This quote is attributed to Socrates and reflects a philosophical concept about the nature of knowledge and wisdom. It suggests that true wisdom lies in acknowledging and recognizing the vastness of what remains unknown. Wisdom is special. Wisdom is beautiful. Wisdom accepts critique and is not prideful. When wisdom recognizes a wrong, she remains humble and graceful, showing intentionality about "getting it right."

Wisdom understands God's love. Wisdom taught me that it is not because of anything that "I" did that caused my blessings. God did not show me signs and wonders, and He certainly didn't show me miracle after miracle for my benefit, but He did so only because He loves me. Humility and wisdom are friends. They are interconnected and woven together like a blanket that gives us comfort. When The Queen showed me my error, I understood the reason I could not find anything after doing some "soul searching". It was because "soul searching" was not required. I was looking in the wrong place; instead, I should have searched my heart.

It was as if the Lord said, "Your soul checks out in good condition, because your soul is anchored in Me. Your mind is rid of clouds. Now, let's take a look at your heart." God was doing a thorough examination of me, like a physician does with his patient. In Matthew 22:37, Jesus says, "Love the Lord your God with all your heart, and with all your soul, and with all your mind." God examined my love; in preparation to perform surgery on me, like a doctor who removes cancer from our vital organs. "Create in me a clean heart, O God, and renew a right spirit within me." Psalm 51:10.

Luke 6:45 "A good man brings good out of the good stored up in his heart, and an evil man brings evil out of the evil stored up in his heart. For out of the abundance of the heart, his mouth speaks." Mark 7:21-23 "For from within, out of the heart of man, come evil thoughts, sexual immorality, theft, murder, adultery, coveting, wickedness, deceit, sensuality, envy, slander, pride, foolishness. All these evil things come from within, and they defile a person." God had reconstructed my mind. He anchored my soul. All He needed to do was put the finishing touches on my heart, to ensure that I was restored back to good spiritual health.

Wisdom was the lifter of my head. Wisdom prevailed.

Reflection Question: **What would God see if He looked into your heart? Take as much time as you need to evaluate what needs to be removed from your heart.**

LIKE FRESH OIL

I healed because "she" deserved it.

"She" Deserved It

Healing was necessary because she deserves the best version of me.

Eight months after the demise of my son, I learned that I was pregnant again with a baby girl. I was incredibly elated and thankful that God had given me another chance to get it right. She was perfect and everything that I needed. I made a promise to God, saying, "I won't mess this up." But I had entered parenthood with an incredible amount of emotional baggage that, at times, I could feel the effects spilling over into how I raised my daughter.

I sometimes used negative words, lacked remorse, or resorted to belittling her when she made a mistake. I was unknowingly damaging her self-image and inflicting the same pain that I once endured on her. I had outbursts of rage that caused her distress. My trauma caused me to be hypervigilant and overprotective, depriving her of the ability to build relationships and interact with her peers. I was emotionally dysregulated, and my unresolved trauma made it difficult to manage my emotions, leading to unpredictable mood swings and excessive withdrawal, which confused her. My trauma had indirectly traumatized my child through my behaviors and emotional state.

One day God showed me myself in her face. At that moment, I realized that if I kept up with this toxic behavior, then I would be passing down a curse that I had acquired generations before, and I refused to do that to my child. God had made me a promise years before her conception. "I will restore what you have lost," and in His faithfulness, He had done just that. Therefore, I was contractually obligated to be the best mother I could be.

I learned how to equip myself with the tools necessary to overcome this generational curse. Healing has allowed me to adopt a completely different parenting style. I do not curse at my child. I allow her to openly and freely express her feelings. She has the right to say "no" and can set boundaries with whomever she wants. I apologize if I am wrong. I do not expect her to stay silent. There is no such thing as staying in a child's place because a child's place has the right to take up space wherever it's needed. I do not force her to hug or to be affectionate with anyone. She can be seen and heard. I consider her feelings when making life choices. I speak life into her and encourage her when she makes mistakes. I let her know every day how proud I am of her. I am intentional about supporting her in whatever phase of life she may be in. I check in on her daily.

Checking in!

It doesn't matter that they laugh

It doesn't matter that they smile

It doesn't matter that they play

It doesn't matter that they look alright

It doesn't matter how well you think you know them

That closet can be full of clothes

Those boxes can hold the most expensive shoes

That toy chest can be full of gadgets

And that snack drawer can be filled with goodies

It doesn't matter…

Check-in on your children.

They live in a time that is totally different from our own. We did not experience what they deal with now.

Check-in on your children.

Be intentional. Be personable. Be genuine. Create a safe space for them; allow them to be their true, authentic self with you. Encourage them. Do away with judgment and harsh criticisms. Be open-minded and flexible. But don't compromise. Be creative in how you check-in. Make it meaningful and specific to each child (If you have more than one). I don't care what else you do, but make time to check-in. Ask all the right questions. And if you don't know what questions to ask, ask God for clarity and wisdom.

They may seem annoyed now, but I promise you, in the end, they will appreciate you for it.

Check-in on your children.

Generational survival is one thing. But let's break the curse. Let's break the cycle. It's time for change, and it starts with you.

Check-in on your children.

My healing journey had a ripple effect on my daughter. The more I healed, so did she. My choosing to heal created a more stable and supportive home environment, which allowed her to become more susceptible to expressing her feelings freely. The more that I actively practiced managing my own emotions, the better equipped I was to respond to her emotional needs with empathy and understanding. Healing taught me how to feel comfortable sharing my experiences with my daughter, and it opened a healthier line of communication that encouraged transparency and vulnerability. Working on my own healing demonstrated to her the importance of self-care, seeking help when needed, and being resilient in the midst of adversity.

I am not that mother who believes that I know everything, because I certainly do not. I listen to what my daughter has to say because she teaches me something new every day. I value her opinion, and I respect her perspective. When I think about it on a deeper level, she sees more clearly than I do because her innocence allows her to view things in a brighter light.

Healing brought me closer to God and gave me a desire to read and study God's Word for myself more diligently. This created a space and opportunity for my daughter and me to dialogue about the scriptures. "Love the Lord your God with all your heart and with all your soul and with all your strength. These commandments that I give you today are to be on your hearts. Impress them on your children. Talk about them when you sit at home and when you walk along the road, when you lie down and when you get up." (Deuteronomy 6:5-7).

I began to teach my daughter how to pray. The Lord had placed it on my heart to print the Lord's Prayer and to tape it on the walls around the house and the refrigerator. She could not go for a drink of water or a slice of cake without looking at His words. I hung one on the wall in the bathroom, so when she sat on the toilet, she studied His words. I was strategic and intentional about building her prayer language. Because one day, our Bibles will be stripped away from us, so I needed His word embedded in her heart. We said it together at night before bed and on car rides. In just one month, my daughter could recite the Lord's Prayer in its entirety verbatim. Tears poured from my face the first time I heard her say it solo. She recited it perfectly.

Our Father, which art in Heaven,

Hallowed be thy name.

Thy kingdom come.

Thy will be done on earth, as it is in Heaven.

Give us this day our daily bread.

And forgive us our trespasses as we forgive those who trespass against us

And lead us not into temptation, but deliver us from evil:

For thine is the kingdom, and the power, and the glory, forever. Amen.

Matthew 6:9-13

My healing and obedience to God's word brought my daughter to salvation, and she definitely deserved that. Train up a child in the way he should go, and when he is old, he will not depart from it. Proverbs 22:6

Reflection Questions: **Who in your life deserves your healing? What actions will you take to heal?**

"SHE" DESERVED IT

Acceptance

"God, grant me the serenity to accept the things I cannot change, the courage to change the things I can, and the wisdom to know the difference."
Serenity Prayer

I don't care what situation you are dealing with; in the midst of it, call the name of Jesus. You can yell it from the mountains, or you can whisper it low, Jesus. He will hear, and He will come to see about you.

Healing requires a full acceptance of past circumstances and intentional creation of new experiences. I was diagnosed with Cicatricial Alopecia in 2017. This form of alopecia causes hair follicles to die off and is replaced by scar tissue, resulting in permanent hair loss. The relaxers that my Mama put in my hair every three months since I was eight years old didn't make it any better. Losing my hair was detrimental to my self-esteem. I became depressed and angry. I went from having a head full of beautiful, thick hair to having thin, brittle, coarse hair; it shed like a dog losing its coat. I was embarrassed when people noticed the bald spots at the crown of my head. I tried to grow my hair, but nothing worked, and the combovers and high buns got redundant. My hair was my glory; it was the thing that made me unique, and when I lost it, I felt like I had lost a part of my identity.

I decided to go natural. The coils of my natural hair help to mask the bald spots. It was hard to embrace at first because I was used to having relaxed hair. I cried often. It was hard for others too, because seeing me with a nappy was out of the ordinary. "Oh, you're having a bad hair day, huh?" On the days I chose to wear twists, I was called "Ms. Celie." The transition from relaxed to natural was challenging. Nobody talks about it. No one discusses the significant texture differences between new growth and relaxed ends, the increased dryness and breakage caused by contrasting textures, the need for a new hair care routine, and the almost impossible task of finding the right product for your hair type. The shrinkage is an entirely separate conversation. Nobody talks about the planning and anxiety associated with wash days.

I was diagnosed with Cervical Cancer in 2022 after a pelvic exam came back with abnormalities. Due to a botched surgery, I have recurring polyps that grow on the lining of my cervix. I must visit my obstetrician every six months to have them removed. Each visit makes my cervix weaker, and my chances of conceiving a child again lessen. I had no quality of life because I bled relentlessly for no reason. My desire to ever be in a relationship was destroyed because intercourse caused me to hemorrhage. I had a distorted perception of myself. "What man would want to deal with the disgusting likes of me?" I thought. I doubted my worth.

Healing brought about a change in me because I began to accept the things that I could not change. I realized that these battles were bigger than me and out of my control. What was the point of exhorting so much energy into these issues? Healing made me realize that I needed to entrust it to God, my Creator, because I have no power to rectify these defects. God is faithful. In His omnipotence, I trust that He will heal and restore me to great health. I practice staying positive and of good cheer because after what Christ went through at Calvary, who am I to complain?

Reflection Questions: **What are some things that you often complain about? What are some things that you know you should let go of?**

ACCEPTANCE

Healing was learning how to protect.

Protection

Protection was what I lacked the most. Growing up, I didn't realize what that void feeling was until I got much older. The hardest thing to cope with was knowing that no one ever made me a priority. No one saw my worth. No one considered me or validated my feelings; no one ever chose me. My mother told me that after she found out about Cravis, she contacted my dad to let him know what had happened. She said that he was very upset and was eager to go after Cravis to punish him for what he had done to me, but she talked him out of it, and he conceded.

I listened to how passionately Mama spoke about Cravis's mother. "I told your Daddy no because I just couldn't do that to her," she said.

The same evening that my mom walked in on Cravis molesting me, she took me to the police station to file an incident report. She said that she had called Uncle to tell him what was going on, and she wanted him to escort us to the police station. I don't remember Uncle being there, but I do remember the big white policeman who asked me all those questions about what Cravis did to me. I was an intelligent kid, and I was able to articulate Cravis's actions well. The officer was impressed that I could use correct terminology like penis, vagina, breast, and buttocks. Those were the words that my mother taught me, so I didn't know any others. I remember how frightening that was for me, as a child, to be speaking to a stranger about my body. I felt very uncomfortable, but I can recall him explaining to me that I was safe with him. It was concluded that no charges could be filed against Cravis because he was still a minor at seventeen.

As far as I could see, my mother had not protected me; she yelled at me and beat me that day. I carried that with me my entire life. I listened as she prioritized his mother's feelings over mine. I couldn't understand how or why she prioritized anybody else's feelings over mine. How come she couldn't see my hurt or feel my pain, but she considered the feelings of my predator's mother? In my view, she had protected them. "As a mother, the only feelings that I would consider in a time like that would be my victimized child's," I thought. When my dad was coming to stand up for me, she convinced him not to. Why? I resented her and him, too, for listening to her because, "A father is supposed to protect his children." That's his God-given obligation and his duty as a man. A man who fails to protect his family is less of a man."

My mother didn't protect me. My father didn't fight for me. My uncles didn't think anything of it. My closest cousin didn't believe me. The law didn't serve me justice. I lacked protection on every hand.

PROTECTION

After the incident with Keith, I spent the remainder of my adolescence in anger. I had always been a cheerful, chipper kid, but not anymore. I walked around with a frown on my face, rolled my eyes, and cringed whenever he entered my presence. I hated being in the house. When my Mama made me get up off the couch and get a job, I said, "You ain't said nothing but a word," because anything to get me out of that house was alright with me.

I wondered why my mother hadn't noticed that my countenance had fallen. Why didn't she see that I was being mean and disrespectful to him? Why didn't she question the change in my behavior? She didn't even ask me why I never slept in my room. Why didn't she ask me if I was okay? Why did she automatically assume that everything was alright just because I had a smile on my face? She would brag about how well she knew her kids. "Girl, I study my kids. I know them like the back of my hand," is what she often said. But I chuckled inwardly because I knew that she didn't know a thing about me. I was crying out for help, a desperate, silent cry. I needed her to hear me, to see me, and I wished that she had heard my silent cries.

It was times when my mother would scold me in discipline, but it was hard for me to take her seriously because, "How dare you try to tell me what's what, like you know everything when you have no clue that your husband is a pedophile." I never said anything like that to my mother because I would never blatantly disrespect her; however, those were my thoughts. I fought silent battles alone, all in the name of protecting her, but there was nobody to protect me.

As a teen, I had become intentional about how I protected myself. I stayed away as much as I could. Between work, spending time with my boyfriend, cheerleading practice, attending school games, and hanging out with my girlfriends, these activities kept me busy. I slept on the couch, close to the front door, just in case I had to make a quick escape. I took showers before my mother left for work because I didn't feel comfortable showering when I was left alone with Keith. It was unfortunate that I had to go through such extreme measures to protect myself. My father's absence didn't make my yearning for protection any better, and as I grew up, I desired it in my relationships. Still, by then, I was so acclimated to abuse that healthy relationships looked abnormal.

I was 26 years old when resentment began to fester. I had always remembered my abuse, but it wasn't until after the birth of my daughter that I realized how traumatized I truly was. Becoming a mother forced me to see things through a different lens, as I was now a mother with the God-given obligation to protect the life of my offspring. This new perspective made me question how I could ever allow anyone to hurt this beautiful child. It wasn't until then that I started to really tap into those secret battles that I fought alone as a child, because I never wanted my daughter to fight those types of battles solo.

I began to think about all the extreme measures I would take to protect her, how I would go to the ends of the world to keep her safe and away from harm and sexual predators. It wasn't until then that I began to dissect every emotion I had suffered. I started to recall my specific behaviors to stay one step ahead of my daughter and recognize them if she ever displayed them. I remembered how lonely and unseen I often felt, and I used that as a tool to recognize her needs.

I was intentional about tapping into every ounce of my motherly instincts. I was intentional about being vigilant. I didn't care about how "sheltered" I kept her because, "what the hell was the other alternative?" There was none. I promised to protect her physically, spiritually, emotionally, mentally, and socially because I didn't see true protection as being anything less than this.

I was so mad and so angry for so long that it clouded my mind and judgment. In my narcissistic and ill mind, I prioritized myself and my own feelings over everyone else's. I did not give an ounce of grace; I only saw my pain.

Healing taught me a deeper meaning. In my pain and my feelings, the definition of retaliation was misconstrued with my desire for protection. She said, "CeCe, I am listening to you, and protection is not what you were expecting. At some point, your need for protection turned into a need for retaliation." My therapist had completely deconstructed my perception of what I thought I needed. Clearly, I had no idea what protection meant because, in my mind, protection was about brawling physically for me.

Healing made me realize that I am no longer the victim, but I am a survivor. Therefore, I no longer needed protection, and any form of protection I thought I needed was dependent on me alone. As a result, I learned how to protect myself and take steps to get out of uncomfortable situations. I learned to:

- Avoid being alone with people I don't know well.

- Trust my gut; if a situation doesn't feel right, say or do whatever is necessary to remove myself.

- Speak firmly when I don't want to do something.

Healing taught me that if I love the Lord, everything will work out for me. On this journey to find a deeper meaning, I referred to the Bible and found some great passages that discussed protection.

- Psalm 91:1-16 "The Lord will deliver you from danger, protect you with his wings, and you will find refuge under him..."

- Psalm 32:7 "God is a hiding place, protects from trouble, and surrounds with shouts of deliverance."

- 2 Thessalonians 3:3 "The Lord is faithful and will guard you against the evil one."

- Exodus 14:14 "The Lord will fight for you, and you shall hold your peace."

To practice positivity and help recondition my mind to be my own protector, I found affirmations and quotes that helped build me up. These are some of my favorites:

"The best protection any woman can have is, courage." Elizabeth Cady Staton

"No one should need to be big enough to destroy others and all of us must have to be powerful and resourceful enough to protect ourselves." Zaman Ali

---

I feel like I'm living in a generation where I'm here to clean up the mess that my elders created—like God called me to be a member of the cleanup crew. I refuse to live in this filth that they created any longer, and I refuse to allow my child to be affected by it, too. The lies, the ignorance, the deception, and the lack of transparency. My pain and my traumas are all direct causes of their dysfunction. But nobody wants to speak about that. The skeletons in the closet, all the filth under the rug; I'm opening the door, and I'm shaking it because it's time. I'm tired! I'm tired of everybody defending the wrong. I'm tired of nobody stepping up and speaking out against wrongdoing. I'm tired of everybody turning a blind eye and not upholding righteousness. I'm tired of it! "Stop snitching," she said. Well, guess what, I'm snitching! Now that I have a life to protect, and if I can also protect the lives of other children in the process, then so be it. But I am no longer keeping silent. And that's my vow to God.

Reflection Questions: What level of protection do you require? Why?

_____
_____
_____
_____
_____
_____
_____
_____
_____
_____
_____
_____
_____
_____
_____
_____
_____
_____
_____
_____

PROTECTION

Forgiveness

"Be kind to one another, tenderhearted, forgiving one another, as God in Christ forgave you."
Ephesians 4:32

I never knew how strong I was until I had to forgive abusers who weren't sorry and accept an apology I never received. This was the absolute hardest challenge in my healing journey because my mind could not comprehend how to forgive, let alone understand the benefits of true forgiveness. It's easy to forgive a person for stepping on your foot or forgetting a birthday, but when I thought about the effects that sexual abuse had on me and the fact that Cravis or Keith never fixed their mouth to say, "I am sorry," forgiveness was the last thing on my mind.

While every sexual abuse survivor's experience impact is unique, I was impacted by *shame*, thinking that I was bad, wrong, dirty, and permanently flawed. *Guilt,* feeling that the abuse was my fault. It was sometimes difficult for me to accurately place the blame. *Denial,* saying things like, "It wasn't that bad. I'm fine. I don't need anything." *Minimizing* the abuse was a coping strategy that included thinking that my abuse was not as bad as someone else's. I often failed to validate the impact of the abuse. I did not know that it was appropriate to be upset, traumatized, or to feel broken.

I had *poor boundaries* because sexual violence is such a boundary violation. It impacted my perception of when and how to set boundaries. I was unfamiliar with boundaries in general, and I had no idea how to create or enforce appropriate boundaries. Sexual abuse is sometimes a betrayal of *trust*; therefore, it was difficult for me to trust other people as well as myself. My sense of *safety* was altered, and my assessment of safe and unsafe situations was distorted. *Isolation* became a big issue, especially when I became an adult. I often felt that I did not deserve support and that others would not want to be my friend. I suffered from repeated cycles of sadness, anger, outbursts of rage, and *hypervigilance*.

In my mind, all these painful emotions had sculpted into a crucifixion that I carried on my back like a complete replica of Jesus headed to Calvary. I bore a cross so heavy and for so long that my flesh began to feel stabbing pains. I would hear people speak about forgiveness as if it were second nature to them. I would shake my head in disagreement because I failed to process in my already ill and narcissistic mind that forgiveness had no prerequisite. I felt like God gave a person like me a pass in not forgiving because if you went to my abusers right now, they would deny that anything happened, let alone admit that they are my perpetrators. "Why would God expect me to forgive a person who has not asked for forgiveness?" Yet, on this journey, I realized that I had an unrealistic expectation of people who do not submit to the will of God, so how ridiculous was it to think for one second that they should apologize? An apology is not a prerequisite for forgiveness.

If you struggle with unforgiveness like I did, be encouraged. "Truly, I tell you, whatever you bind on earth will be bound in heaven, and whatever you loose on earth will be loosed in heaven. "Again, truly, I tell you that if two of you on earth agree about anything they ask for, it will be done for them by my Father in heaven. For where two or three gather in my name, there am I with them." Then Peter came to Jesus and asked, "Lord, how many times shall I forgive my brother or sister who sins against me? Up to seven times?" Jesus answered, "I tell you, not seven times, but seventy-seven times." Matthew 18:18-22.

We may be offended when people speak of forgiveness because we can never get back the tears, and we will never get back the time that we lost. When we forgive somebody, we give ourselves the gift of peace, freedom, and rest. If you feel like you are obligated to hold on to this person, ask yourself, is the blood of Jesus enough to pay for what they did? Is what Jesus did on Calvary sufficient to take away the sin that they committed against you? You may never regain your innocence, but the cross of Christ is surely enough to pay for that offense, and to believe otherwise is like an offense against the cross, as if to say, 'Lord, your blood was not strong enough to pay for my pain.

Our Lord hung on a cross pleading, "Father, forgive them, for they know not what they do." The Lord knows things about us, things that we did in our past. He knows that we are human, and He gives us grace daily. God knew that in times of weakness, we would struggle with forgiveness. He knew that it would seem almost impossible for us to forgive. Many of us continue to harbor unforgiveness in our hearts towards others, but the Lord, in His infinite mercy, has given us teachings and perfect examples of grace and strength. God understood that it would be impossible not to get hurt in this life, that we would be broken so severely and stripped of the capacity to forgive. However, the Lord left us His words and knowledge to guide us in how to respond to people when we are wounded.

I was molested at four, five, six, seven, and eight years old. I will never be able to get that time back. I learned how to accept the things that I cannot change and that forgiveness was not for my abusers, but forgiveness was for me to be set free; it was to get out of the prison that I had been in in my mind for thirty years. True forgiveness is boundless. Whenever I thought of the pain, I had to forgive them over and over and over again. As I practiced forgiveness, it became effortless because I began to accept that unforgiveness was a sin. But I craved for a deeper understanding, and in that, I learned not to keep count of the number of times I forgave them, because God, my Savior, does not keep count of my faults. In my season of trauma, in the moments of betrayal, I challenged myself to let it all go.

It's not the outside that defines a man, but his heart. Hurt people hurt people, and mess begot mess. Keith's and Cravis's hearts were filled with trifling calamity, so much that it seeped out their pores like foul perspiration, and I finally comprehended that only God possesses the power to deal with that level of mess.

In therapy, the topic of discussion for the week was forgiveness. She knew how much I struggled with it. She asked me to make a list of things I needed to forgive myself of. This assignment was challenging and almost impossible for me to complete, but I persevered and came up with some ideas that I felt made sense. She asked me to grab a pencil and a highlighter and read my list out loud. The conversation went like this:

Me: I need to forgive myself for the way that I have coped with my abuse.

Her: Take your pencil and put an X on that one. You're X'ing this one because your coping mechanisms were a trauma response. Keep going.

Me. I need to forgive myself for becoming so depressed.

Her: X that one. Depression is a trauma response. Keep going.

Me: I need to forgive that I have allowed these men to take power over my mind and feelings.

Her: Losing your power is a part of trauma. Put an X on that one. Continue.

Me: I need to forgive myself for wanting revenge.

Her: Grab your highlighter and highlight this one. This is one that you need to be actively working on. Very good. Let's keep going.

Me: I need to forgive myself for being so angry and full of rage.

Her: X that one. Anger and rage are normal trauma responses.

Me: I need to forgive myself for the suicidal thoughts.

Her: X. Suicidal thoughts can occur when people have been traumatized. Keep going.

Me: I need to forgive that I allowed so much time to pass with negative mental consumptions.

Her: Avoidance is a normal trauma response. X that one.

Me: I need to forgive myself for not speaking out or saying no.

Her: X that one too. Children cannot give or deny consent. You literally lacked the ability to say no because you were a child and under duress. Avoidance is a normal trauma response. Continue.

Me: I need to forgive myself for being everyone's gatekeeper because my silence has protected my abusers.

Her: Good, highlight that one. You should be actively working on this. You can no longer be anyone else's gatekeeper but your own. You can no longer be silent about your abuse. Now is your time to speak out. Do you have any more?

Me: Yes, I have one more. I need to forgive myself for being scared and afraid.

Her: X that one. Being scared and afraid are both normal trauma responses.

She had, in a very creative approach, made me identify what needed forgiveness versus what were normal reactions to my trauma. A trauma response is a natural involuntary reaction to a traumatic event, while forgiveness is a conscious decision to release resentment and negativity regarding the traumatic event. Forgiveness is not always necessary for healing, but in my instance, it was because I had clearly identified two issues that needed direct attention. The X's were not because I had listed anything wrong, but they were an indicator that I had done everything right. I displayed a normal response to my trauma. By the time we were finished with this activity, I had soiled about eight tissues.

Reflection Questions: **Is there anyone in your life with whom you struggle to forgive? Who? Why? Do you have a desire to forgive them? Why or why not?**

FORGIVENESS

Healing is showing the world who I really am.

Showing the World Who I Really Am

Healing is displaying the evidence of the goodness of God.

"You are one of the hardest working Queens I've ever seen, the backbone of our family. Everything you do for your family is greatly appreciated and can never go unnoticed. You're doing the absolute best job raising your child, and doing it with ease. Happy Mother's Day. Bro."

"To my beautiful sister. Happy birthday. You are truly a blessing to me, my family, and so many others. Words cannot express how thankful and grateful I am to have you as a friend. You are more than that, my sister. Thank you for allowing me to be a safe space and sharing your life with me. I want you to always remember that I see you, I hear you, I love you. God took his time with you, and I can't wait for the world to see more of you. Nieka"

Many people around me see greatness, but I did not always see greatness in myself. But even with self-doubt and a lack of esteem, I still knew that I was different, that I was set apart from others. It was something that God instilled in me before I was born. I have always been favored by people and, most importantly, by God. God, in His perfect wisdom, had placed something in me before my conception. He planted it, watered it, and watched it grow.

It was kinda strange growing up and knowing that I was different. At times, I fought against it, and at other times, I fought to embrace it. I didn't want it. I wanted to be like the rest of them. I didn't want to be meek; I wanted to be that girl who told people off and didn't have any qualms about doing so. I wanted to be an extrovert. I tried to be that person, but even in my stupidity, God kept His hand over me. He kept me from all seen and all unseen danger. He encamped angels on both sides of me to protect me from myself.

Yet, I was a silent watcher. It seemed as if silence was a gift given to me by God because in my silence was my ability to discern, and in my silence was my ability to hear. I cherished silence, and I learned how to move in silence. "People don't know that you love God," Bishop whispered in my ear. When he spoke those words, I chuckled inwardly because I understood the spiritual significance behind them. God had indeed silenced me because He was doing a profound work within me, but it wasn't time for it to be released. He concealed me, covered me, and made me nearly invisible. It sometimes bothered me that folks thought that I was ignorant of the Word. They had no idea that I was no longer drinking milk but was eating meat. It was kinda like Jesus, who didn't start his mission until He was thirty. God had taken His time to put inside Jesus everything He wanted Him to have, to be able to save the world, and He packed it away until the time was right. This is how God did with me. He took his time with me, putting in me everything that I needed until He was ready to show me off to the world—everything in God's time.

A Time for Everything
Ecclesiastes 3:1-11

3 There is a time for everything,
and a season for every activity under the heavens:

² a time to be born and a time to die,
a time to plant and a time to uproot,
³ a time to kill and a time to heal,
a time to tear down and a time to build,
⁴ a time to weep and a time to laugh,
a time to mourn and a time to dance,
⁵ a time to scatter stones and a time to gather them,
a time to embrace and a time to refrain from embracing,
⁶ a time to search and a time to give up,
a time to keep and a time to throw away,
⁷ a time to tear and a time to mend,
a time to be silent and a time to speak,
⁸ a time to love and a time to hate,
a time for war and a time for peace.

⁹ What do workers gain from their toil? ¹⁰ I have seen the burden God has laid on the human race. ¹¹ He has made everything beautiful in its time.

When my time came, I struggled. In the wave of emotions, I struggled with whether people would take me seriously because they would know my past and judge me accordingly. I struggled with whether people would understand my message altogether; I struggled with finding the courage. I worried about what my friends and family would say about me speaking so openly about my abuse and my past. But The Lord, in His boundless glory, knew what I needed.

CeCe,

You are special to me. There is nothing that can change how I feel about you. You are mine, and I love you so much. I have got you. I am covering you on every side. I'm there even when you don't feel like I'm there. Believe in me and know that I can't fail. I CAN'T FAIL. You will overcome, and you have favor. My favor is with you. What I have for you, nobody else can have it. The portion that is yours is yours. Rest in me. Lean on me. Trust in me. I am the peace you need. I am all you need. Spend time with me. I've got you. Healing belongs to you!! You are mine, and I am yours. I am near.

Thus say the Lord!!
God.
10/27/2024

God had performed yet another miracle. He had miraculously written this letter to me through the hands of a stranger to exhort and encourage me in a moment of doubt. God had manifested His Spirit to operate through the hands of an unfamiliar man, giving me the reassurance I needed to do a work that was exceedingly more than I could ever imagine. He purposely wrote me this letter to lift my head and to build back up the confidence that Satan had torn down. This letter anchored me back to God. I was instantly brought back into covenant with God. In humble prayer I became like the Pharisee man who stood and prayed saying, "God, I thank you that I am not like the others." Luke 18:11. He continues to show Himself real and true to me. I am divinely favored, I am different, and I am grateful. Healing has brought out the best in me because it brought out what God put in.

Reflection Questions: **What are some things that you want to accomplish in this season? Think big. How can you be intentional about manifesting them?**

_____
_____
_____
_____
_____
_____
_____
_____
_____
_____
_____
_____
_____
_____
_____
_____
_____
_____
_____
_____

SHOWING THE WORLD WHO I REALLY AM

Healing was understanding that now "I" am held to a higher standard.

Higher Standards

"When they go low, we go high."
Michelle Obama

Cravis. I hate you. There are two people in this world that I hate, and you are one of them. I have lived thirty-four years hating you, and nothing will change how I feel. I don't believe that God expects me to love my abusers, and I certainly don't think that God expects me to forgive those who don't ask for forgiveness. How can I? You are a monster, a predator, and a sneaking conniving snake. Your soul deserves to burn in hell because you have hidden your sin while impersonating a godly man. You are horrible, and everything you touch will fall!

In my brokenness, this was my truth, and these were my sentiments. Resentment and strife had snatched me up in a whirlwind, and hatred became effortless. This hatred was complicated because it was deeply rooted in my past; it festered over time, it was septic, and it injured me, which made it difficult to heal. But not impossible because with God, all things are possible.

Healing had a way of softening my heart because I placed God before me and I made Him my priority. In my journey, I asked Him to take the lead. God knows all things; therefore, He knew the things that consumed me the most, and He knew how to pluck them out.

I dreamt that I was standing in a souvenir store on an island that sat next to the ocean. I shopped around for trinkets and goodies. Suddenly, everyone in the store stopped in amazement as they gazed outside at the rain that poured onto the island. When I looked outside, crystals, jewels, and rhinestones sparkled like perfect teardrops falling from the sky. I walked outside to the ocean's edge, looking out at thousands of people in the water. They were waiting for me. People hung onto the ledge of the water to get as close to me as they could. Some people stood around as spectators. I began to proclaim the goodness of Jesus in my own unique way. The words that I spoke were relatable. The people were fascinated by my dramatizations.

They smiled, and they laughed in good cheer. They received me. A black woman who sat at a picnic table yelled out, "But I don't believe in Jesus!" I looked at her, and before I could say anything, a white man interjected. He began to explain to her why she should believe in Jesus. When the white man had finished talking, a black man began to explain why she should believe in Jesus. He was theatrical and used props to illustrate his point of view. As I looked around, I saw thousands of people who had congregated both in the waters and on the shore. The atmosphere was filled with a spirit of creativity while trying to convince this woman to believe. Within my dream, I received a revelation that God had used my presence and platform to bring all these people together, and that my ministry was carried out in a down-to-earth and creative way. The effort to get this woman to believe was the ultimate act of goodness.

God is raising up a generation of believers who strive for a deeper understanding. The Bible speaks about how God calls people to a higher standard than the world and to raise their standards by living in accordance with God's will. Romans 12:2 teaches us, "Do not be conformed to the pattern of the world but be transformed by the renewing of your mind." God's standards are the ultimate measure of goodness. In my efforts to become good, my behaviors, words, responsibilities, parenting, practices, mindset, potential, expectations, and purpose are being held to a higher standard.

In God's promise, "I will restore what you have lost," was the need to pluck hatred out of my heart, to restore the love that was lost, and to replenish me with, mercy, and kindness. "The Lord had appeared of old unto me, saying, Yea, I have loved thee with an everlasting love: therefore, with lovingkindness have I drawn thee." Jeremiah 31:2-4. To become more like Christ, I became intentional about displaying lovingkindness.

Cravis. I do not hate you, but I will continue to pray for strength as I strive every day to love you more and more through faith. God is doing a work in me that is much more rewarding than hating you. I choose freedom; therefore, I choose to forgive you. I choose to walk in any room at any time with my head held high because you have not broken me. I am a child of the King; I will adjust my crown and move forward. I want my reward in the Kingdom. I deserve it. I will continue to uphold a standard that surpasses all the trauma that you inflicted on me. I will continue to pray for you.

God is raising up a standard…

In a vision, God showed me standing in the middle of a huge football stadium. It was filled with people in the risers, and it thundered with roars of applause and cheers as the people watched Jesus being lifted up on the cross. I watched in agony and wondered why the people cheered because this surely was no cheerful matter. As I was coming out of the vision, I heard the voice of Jesus bellow in wrath, *"THEY ARE MAKING A MOCKERY OF ME!"*

People are disrespectful and intentionally making fun of Jesus, treating His existence and teachings with disgust, often through words or actions showing a blatant disregard for his power and his authority. They are making a spectacle of Him even inside the churches.

I used to attend a church that had become so well known it had the potential to become a mega-church because the teachings and the flow of the ministry were just that good. People traveled far and wide to attend the services. You could easily trust that this pastor had indeed spent time with the Lord because his teachings were prolific, his revelations were spot on, and his sermons were so perfectly executed that every Sunday, people came to the altar to give their lives to Jesus. As years passed, he was exposed for having an inappropriate sexual relationship with a minor. His secrets and deceit corrupted this church.

I attended a church where the moment you walked in, you felt the presence of God. The people were kind and friendly, and over time, they became like family. My mother became an active part of the ministry. The pastor allowed her to teach and began to build her platform within the church. Some years later, we learned that the pastor was secretly having an affair with another woman at the church, whom we believed to be his daughter. This was heartbreaking because we trusted him, we looked up to him for spiritual guidance, and we admired the pastor and first lady's relationship. The hypocrisy of that pastor led many church members astray.

One day, I visited a church with my mother. I was seven months pregnant with my son. The pastor of this church was a middle-aged woman. I sat and listened to her message. Towards the end of the service, she began to speak to me. She asked if she could touch my protruding pregnant belly. In my ignorance, I allowed it. As she held my belly, she spoke about all the blessings my son would acquire, how he would be a good child, and how he would preach and spread the gospel. But, two weeks later, I learned that my son had died in my loins. This woman had spoken a lie over me and into the life of my son, a false "prophet."

This is a problem with some churches today; they lack true reverence, truth, biblical teachings, love, and grace. But God is raising up a standard of people who desire and require to be in the presence of God and take His word seriously. Galatians 6:7. "Do not be deceived, God is not mocked, for whatever a man sows, that he will also reap." Therefore, God will not allow Himself to be treated with contempt or ridiculed.

Spiritual manipulation is a form of control that undermines someone's ability to think or act independently. It involves using scripture and spiritual language to gain power and control over others, often through deception, guilt tripping, and intimidation. In times like these, it is important to pray for spiritual stamina. This is also why it's crucial to study Gods Word for yourself; study to show yourself approved. The next time you are succumbing to spiritual manipulation say this, "Excuse me ma'am/sir, I have my own relationship with God. You are not the only one He speaks to. So, if He ever needed to share that type of information with me, about me, He would. I have direct access to Him, and He has access to me. Stop with the spiritual manipulation. I'm beyond that. I'm wiser than you know."

God is raising up a generation of seers…

Acts 2:17 "'In the last days, God says, I will pour out my Spirit on all people. Your sons and daughters will prophesy, your young men will see visions, your old men will dream dreams."

"Mommy, I had a dream. I dreamt that a man came into our house. But he didn't try to harm us. He started pouring oil all over the floor, and you came with a bottle to protect me, but he was not there to hurt me."

It was only through spiritual eyes that I was able to see this miracle because I struggled with the title of this book. I believe by faith that God gave my nine-year-old daughter this dream to confirm the title and to encourage me to keep writing. To share my story with the world, to reassure me, and let me know that I got it right. God is faithful.

"Mommy, I had a dream. I dreamed that we were at Walmart, the one near our house. We were standing in the parking lot talking to some people, but the people were bad. Then, a tornado came and destroyed those people. But the tornado didn't hurt us. You and I just walked home." This was a dream shared with me by my daughter. Two weeks later, an EF3 tornado ripped through the city of St. Louis, unexpectedly destroying the land.

"If my people who are called by my name humble themselves and pray and seek my face and turn from their wicked ways, then I will hear from heaven and will forgive their sin and heal their land." 2 Chronicles 7:14.

Raise her up, oh Lord, raise her up.

Reflection Questions: What are things that you hold to a high standard? What standards can God hold you to?

HIGHER STANDARDS

Healing was proclaiming that I am free.

Proclaiming that I am Free

If I fail to do this part, then this entire book was written in vain. We are living in the last days. If you are not already connected to God, now is the time, because today is almost over, and tomorrow is not promised. A life with God is necessary, and the road to Christ is simple. If you do not know God or do not have a personal relationship with Jesus, you can change that right now. If you desire a relationship with Jesus, confess this short prayer.

Lord, I have chosen to turn away from sin.
I believe that Jesus Christ is the Son of God,
I believe that Jesus died on the cross for my sins and was risen in three days. (Romans 10:9)
Come into my heart and be my personal Lord and Savior.

It is that simple! Welcome to freedom!

There is a difference between believing in Christ and living for Christ. Believing in Christ is a heartfelt trust and reliance on Him. It is acknowledging His existence and agreeing with Christian principles. It involves a personal recognition that Jesus is the Son of God, our Savior. Belief is a steadfast knowing in His finished works at the Cross. Belief is the first step.

I remember having a conversation with my uncle. The conversation wasn't about anything deep or heavy, but he said something that completely changed my perspective on believing in Christ. He said, "I really don't understand why people choose not to believe. I mean, people purchase insurance policies for those 'just in case' moments. So, why not believe in Christ, 'just in case' He is real?"

Living for Christ requires a high level of discipline, but it can certainly be achieved with time, diligence, patience, and self-control. It leads to a process of transformation, where believers are gradually conformed to the image of Christ. It requires a deeper level of understanding and a desire for a renewed mindset. Living for Christ means intentionally striving to follow God's example through service and sharing the message of Jesus with those who have not heard it.

I remember there was a time when I ran from God, because I didn't want to do the work and I certainly didn't want to make the sacrifice. I knew my gifts, but I deserted them. I was afraid of the unfamiliar, and conversations about God made me feel uncomfortable. My level of sin made me feel unworthy; shame and embarrassment kept me from witnessing even a glimpse of my purpose. Sin was my choice. Sin was my comfort. Sin was my friend. Sin was more pleasing to my flesh.

But, on this journey, I chose to turn away from sin when I realized that my sin made me no different from my abusers.

"Therefore, no condemnation now exists for those in Christ Jesus, because the Spirit's law of life in Christ Jesus has set you free from the law of sin and of death. What the law could not do since it was limited by the flesh, God did. He condemned sin in the flesh by sending His own Son in the likeness of ours, under sin's domain, and as a sin offering, so that the law's requirement would be fulfilled in us who do not walk according to the flesh but according to the Spirit. For those who live according to the flesh, think about the things of the flesh, but those who live according to the Spirit, about the things of the Spirit. For the mindset of the flesh is death, but the mindset of the Spirit is life and peace. For the mindset of the flesh is hostile to God because it does not submit itself to God's law, for it is unable to do so. Those who are in the flesh cannot please God. You, however, are not in the flesh, but in the Spirit, since the Spirit of God lives in you. But if anyone does not have the Spirit of Christ, he does not belong to Him. Now if Christ is in you, the body is dead because of sin, but the Spirit is life because of righteousness. And if the Spirit of Him who raised Jesus from the dead lives in you, then He who raised Christ from the dead will also bring your mortal bodies to life through His Spirit who lives in you."
(Romans 8:1-11)

Reflection Questions: How do you feel right now? What are some sinful acts that you can be intentional about turning away from? What steps can you take to stay away from that sin?

_____

_____

_____

_____

_____

_____

_____

_____

_____

_____

_____

_____

_____

_____

_____

_____

_____

_____

_____

_____

PROCLAIMING THAT I AM FREE

Healing was witnessing God put it all together.

Witnessing God

"He is a master craftsman, expert in working with gold, silver, and bronze. He is skilled in engraving and mounting gemstones and in carving wood. He is a master in every craft!"
Exodus 31:4-5 NLT

This book is a miracle because it completes a work that God had performed in a total of 365 days. God took the time to feed me every word to put into this book, gentle whispers in my ear. I always knew that I would write a book because I knew that my story was relevant and worth sharing to help others or raise awareness. Sometimes I doubted my ability, and fear hindered me. I worried about what others would say. I never knew when it would happen or what it would consist of, but I knew that when it happened, God would lead and direct me.

My greatest moves were done in silence to prevent slanders and negativity from naysayers. God gave me clarity and a clear heart to release my story. I worked diligently with a professional to help build my confidence and mental stamina to withstand potential rejections and criticisms. Every chapter in this book is a testament to God's love for me, his faithfulness, and His unmerited favor. My Lord has kept His hand of protection over me, and as a show of gratitude, I give Him my life. Without Him, I am nothing.

Writing was my outlet; it's what I did to escape the world, but it faded away with life's ebbs and flows. It wasn't until now that I got it back, when I went on my healing journey. On this journey, I found the missing link and was given the substance to restore the broken apparatus that enabled me to function. You see, an apparatus is a complex structure within a system, or the equipment needed for a particular purpose. With wear and tear comes deterioration, and it soon will lack proper functioning. But, on this journey, I discovered that the apparatus was not permanently broken; it just needed oil for restoration.

"Lord, allow me to be your apparatus. I am a willing vessel. Use me as you see fit, and when my parts become rusted and worn, caress the crevices with your oil. In the name of Jesus. Amen."

"These tears that you see streaming down my face, please don't consider them tears of sadness, but these are tears of pure joy, like fresh oil."

This book is compiled of material that the Lord had supernaturally pieced together like a puzzle. He miraculously assembled scriptures, sermons, research papers, notes from my counselor trainee program, an admissions essay, greeting cards, journal entries, dreams, conversations, and prayers. He flooded me with revelations, ideas, and memories as I spent countless hours reading my Bible. God spoke to me throughout the night. I slept with a pen and notebook next to my bed because I was frequently woken up and filled with words. I became stronger mentally, spiritually, and emotionally. God himself had put me on a wheel and began to mold me. He was the potter, and I was the clay, and I delighted in every turn. Jeremiah 18.

When God promised me that He would restore everything that I have lost, He superseded my expectations, and He continues to do so.

I thoroughly enjoyed writing this book; it was a journey. I put my sweat and tears into making it and spent a great deal of time with God. Some things I struggled with because I knew that if I published these words, then the world would be able to hold me accountable. I travailed, but God gave me courage and a desire to tell my story, my truth; I was determined to give birth to this thing. It's like this book is my new accountability partner, and it forces me to uphold every word that I put in it. To keep going, to keep trusting, to keep the faith, to stay disciplined, to keep forgiving, to keep loving, to stay positive, to set boundaries, to protect myself, to continue to heal.

God had brought me to my knees so deeply that I had no other choice but to seek help. God had purposely removed people from my life to allow me to be able to spend more time with Him, because I had put so much time and energy into men who pretended to love me. The type of love I sought so desperately for, I failed to realize, only existed in Christ. It was as if God had become selfish with me; He wanted me all to Himself, and I had reached a point where I was alright with that.

I sought professional help. I actively attended therapy and was intentional about doing the work to heal. I never missed a meeting. I put my all into it. It was as if I had enrolled myself in school again. I carried books, and I read them diligently. I did my writing and completed my workbooks. I was open and honest. I poured out my heart to my therapist, and she poured out her heart to me. It was several times that I saw the tears well up in her eyes at the words I spoke, the Lord was speaking through me. I exceeded her expectations so much that she encouraged me to pursue a career in counseling. She said that she saw something in me that she had never seen in a client in all her years as a counselor. I took her advice and applied for graduate school; a second master's degree. I was accepted into the Master of Arts program in mental health counseling with ease. My healing journey inspired me to help others on their own healing journey.

I joined a local community church after learning the importance of placing myself under authority. I needed to sit under sound doctrine and receive spiritual counsel too. I needed to develop discipline, and I desperately desired to be surrounded by other Christians who shared my same values and beliefs. They became my friends. God had restored my circle of friends with people who have power and a purpose.

I became stronger in prayer. I knew about prayer, I had always understood its importance, but I never put it into action to the point where I came out expecting a miracle. Prayer became something like my daily bread. Prayer became my way of staying connected to God. Just as I would pick up the phone and text a friend to say hello, I went to God in the same way. We had built a relationship. My Lord became my best friend. Prayer wasn't just something I did when I wanted something, but it became mandatory. It was not one thing that I asked the Lord for that He did not do for me. Our faithfulness to one another became evident. He poured into me everything that I needed to heal my wounds. He poured into me, like fresh oil.

You don't know the cost of the oil!

The link between oil and the Holy Spirit is profound. Anointed oil is a representation of the Holy Spirit, and it symbolizes divine presence, joy, abundance and godly favor. Hebrews 1:9 states: "You have loved righteousness and hated lawlessness; therefore God, Your God, has anointed You with the oil of gladness above your companions."

The oil carries a fervent significance in Scripture, particularly in the context of leadership, sanctification, and divine purpose. Exodus 29:7 asserts, "Then you shall take the oil, pour it upon his head, and anoint him." This command was given from God to Moses concerning Aaron, as a symbol of transformation and being set apart for a holy purpose.

The oil was a mixture of spices, and a sacred concoction designed specifically for a purpose (Exodus 30:23-25). was not merely olive oil, but it was infused with divine significance, representing the presence of God, the empowerment by His Spirit, and the impartation of His authority.

When we are anointed with the oil, we are chosen to intercede on behalf of the people, to represent them before God, and to lead them in worship. The act of anointing demonstrates God's desire to involve humanity in His divine plan. The oil became a significant substance, illustrating how God intentionally weaves His purpose into the fabric of human existence.

When we accept Jesus Christ as our personal Lord and Savior, we are anointed with the holy oil by faith and sealed with the Holy Spirit a promise until the day of redemption. When we ask Jesus to come into our lives, we must trust in His finished works at the cross. The moment that you believe that your faith is not strong enough is the moment that trouble stirs up because you doubt that Jesus' blood shed on the cross was not enough. Be encouraged, for the prayers of a righteous man will be answered.

I am healed through Christ because of His blood on the cross. Healing has brought me happiness, joy, and a peace that I never knew existed, a peace that surpasses all understanding.

I questioned how oil is extracted from an olive. I discovered that an olive is first crushed into a paste. The paste then undergoes a process called "pressing" to separate the liquid from the solid. The extracted liquid is then separated in a process that allows the oil to rise to the top. The resulting oil is then filtered to remove solids or sediments.

The Garden of Gethsemane is located on the Mount of Olives near Jerusalem. This is the place where Jesus went to pray just before He was betrayed, arrested and crucified. Research suggests that the Mount of Olives was an oil press and was equipped with an apparatus to press oil. There, Jesus experienced intense anguish as He prayed relentlessly to His Father, seeking relief from the suffering He knew was coming. Scripture articulates that Jesus prayed so intensely that His sweat became like drops of blood. Ultimately, Jesus surrendered to the will of His Father. Mathew 26:36-46.

There is a spiritual symbolism and direct correlation between the process of oil being pressed from an olive and the anguish that Jesus endured. They both require processes of intense pressure and extraction. This process serves as a profound example as Jesus suffered with the weight of the sins of the world pressing on Him. But, just as olives produce oil, Jesus' suffering on The Cross produced grace, blessings, mercy, and forgiveness for humanity.

The pressure that I endured in my life does not compare to the pressure that Christ Jesus endured. How dare I complain?

The greatest thing about our minds and our imaginations is that they will allow us to go wherever we desire. In my mind, I accompanied Jesus up the Mount of Olives and followed him into the Garden of Gethsemane. I sat with Him. I listened as He conversed with the Father in a tone of humble cries. He pleaded to The Father for mercy. Yet, He understood His assignment and that His pain would breed a purpose. I trailed them up the mountain and witnessed His persecution. I positioned myself prostrate before the King in sovereign worship as Christ my Lord hung on the Cross at Calvary. I watched as His sinless body was beaten, then catastrophically punctured by a spear that caused His blood to splatter, saturating all who watched with sympathy, how humbling is the privilege of His blood to fall fresh on me because I laid at His feet. I caressed every crevice of my body with His blood, like fresh oil.

Oh, My Lord, My God, thank you for the oil!

Reflection Questions: **What makes life meaningful for you? What do you stand for, even when it's uncomfortable or unpopular? What are your guiding principles in life? What are you willing to struggle for because it's worth it?**

LIKE FRESH OIL

Words from the Author

There is a reason why storytelling is so powerful. It's because when we share our stories, we share a piece of ourselves with the world, which makes our existence relevant. When we do that, it can be incredibly healing for our mental health and revitalizing to our spirits.

When I started telling my story, I only intended to write it down for myself, but God, in his omnipotence, had a greater plan. He knew that disclosure would be my breakthrough because silence had me captive for far too long. In His profound glory, God made it evident that through my humble obedience, many people would be healed, and lives would draw closer to Christ.

I challenge you to break the silence. Tell your story because the world needs to hear it.

Allow God to heal you, to restore your brokenness, then become His mouthpiece.

There is power in your story!

> *"Be strong and courageous. Do not be afraid or terrified because of them, for the LORD your God goes with you; He will never leave you nor forsake you."*
> Deuteronomy 31:6-8

About the Author

Ceairia LaShay Perry, better known as CeCe, was born and raised in St. Louis, Missouri. She is a proud graduate of the St. Louis Public School District, Beaumont High School. After achieving her high school diploma with honors, CeCe went on to pursue a bachelor's degree in criminal justice with a focus in juvenile justice from Harris-Stowe State University. Her value for education influenced her decision to pursue a master's degree in legal studies and paralegal certification from Webster University.

CeCe's love for humanity and devout commitment to God, catapulted her mission to help people understand how to heal through reconciliation, and the power of prayer. Her personal encounters helped sculpt an awareness for personal growth and propelled into a desire to assist others in reclaiming mental health. Ceairia, is currently pursuing a master's degree in mental health counseling at Webster University.

Her graceful poise, and authenticity in story writing captures the essence of who she really is.

References

Bancroft, Lundy. (2003). *Why Does He Do That? Inside the Minds of Angry and Controlling Men.*

Bass, Ellen & Davis, Laura. (2008). *The Courage to Heal: A Guide for Women Survivors of Child Sexual Abuse. 4th Edition, 20th anniversary edition.*

McKay, Matthew & Sutker, Catherine. (2005). *The Self-Esteem Guided Journal: A 10-Week Program.*

Thomas Nelson New King James Version: Super Giant Print Reference Bible, 2013.